ABILITY INNOVATION

ABILITY INNOVATION

THE FUTURE OF HOUSING FOR PEOPLE WITH INTELLECTUAL & DEVELOPMENTAL DISABILITIES NATIONWIDE

ASTRI DOUB

NDP

NEW DEGREE PRESS

COPYRIGHT © 2019 ASTRI DOUB

ABILITY INNOVATION

The Future of Housing for People with Intellectual & Developmental Disabilities Nationwide

ISBN   978-1-64137-307-4   *Paperback*

             978-1-64137-594-8   *Ebook*

Dedicated to my brothers, Robb and Poe

CONTENTS

INTRODUCTION

Robb is my older brother.

He is a swimmer, bowler, horseback rider, and music appreciator.

He is one of very few people who I know will be completely honest about whether he is happy to see me, and he is the only person with whom I feel comfortable singing at the top of my lungs to bluegrass music in the car.

He is also nonverbal and has autism and Down Syndrome, but he is not defined by his intellectual and developmental disabilities (IDD).Like the other seven billion people living on the planet, Robb is an individual made up of complexities, contradictions, and late-night cravings for hot dogs with ketchup.

**

The American Association on Intellectual and Developmental Disabilities (AAIDD) defines IDD in this way: "Intellectual disability is a disability characterized by significant limitations in both intellectual functioning and in adaptive behavior, which covers many everyday social and practical skills. This disability originates before the age of 18."[1]

How many people in the United States live with intellectual and/or developmental disabilities? Answering this question is trickier than you might think. You can look at the results of the 2010 census, which reported 1.2 million adults with intellectual disabilities, 944,000 adults with developmental disabilities, and 1.7 million children with IDD.[2] Those figures total 3.84 million, but the professionals who provide services to those within the population of people with IDD know that these figures are a gross underestimate.If you want more accurate data, you have to collect it from all the different state agencies who serve this population. It's an incredibly complex task, but there are a couple of groups who have risen to the challenge. The "State of the States in Intellectual and Developmental Disabilities" is a project run by the University

---

1   "Definition of Intellectual Disability ." *American Association on Intellectual and Developmental Disabilities,* 2019.

2   "Census: More Americans Have Disabilities – Disability Scoop." *Disability Scoop,* 2012.

of Colorado with support from the Administration on Intellectual and Developmental Disabilities, and it examines spending on housing and program trends for people with IDD in every state nationwide. The most recent 2017 edition revealed that there are over 5 million people living with IDD.[3]

**

Most people hear about children with IDD through the media. Some of these stories cover how public schools struggle when figuring out how to best serve students with IDD.[4] The more popular stories are the uplifting ones like the water boy with autism who played in his senior basketball game or the girl with Down Syndrome who sang a duet with a homeless man.[5]

What many people fail to understand or choose to ignore is that the children in these stories will grow up to become adults one day.

3   Braddock, David, Laura Haffer, Richard Hemp, Emily Shea Tanis, and Jiang Wu. *The State of the States in Intellectual and Developmental Disabilities: 2017.* 2017.

4   Otterman, Sharon. "Schools Struggle Over How To Teach Severely Disabled People." *The New York Times, 2017.*

5   Merrill, Elizabeth. "The Game Nobody Could Forget." *ESPN,* 2016. "Heart Warming Moment – Homeless Man And Girl With Down Syndrome.". *ZOFA ViralWorld,* January 31, 2019.

There are 2.45 million adults with IDD in the US.[6] My brother Robb is now 19. Adulthood is approaching fast.

However, I was not thinking about Robb's future in the summer of 2018. They were the months between my sophomore and junior years of high school, and I was eating, sleeping, and breathing all things collegiate in an effort to narrow down my list of potential schools. That's why when my mom said my dad and I would be going on a tour, I thought she meant that it would just be another college tour for me. Even though I discovered the truth only a couple seconds later, I still felt jolted by the reality of the situation.

We were going to tour Pathfinder Village, a community for adults with IDD, somewhere Robb might be able to live as an adult.

This was going to be my first tour to see an option for Robb's future, and I was sure I would be in tears throughout it. We had heard Pathfinder Village was one of the best places in the country, but the better it was, the more painful it would make our situation. First off, a more than five-hour drive from our home would be too far for us to live from Robb. Also, Medicaid benefits do not transfer to other states, so

---

6   Braddock, David, Laura Haffer, Richard Hemp, Emily Shea Tanis, and Jiang Wu. *The State of the States in Intellectual and Developmental Disabilities: 2017.* 2017.

my parents would have needed to take on an unimaginable economic burden.

On average, new college graduates are saddled with $30,00-$40,000 in student loan debt for four years of higher education.

Community living homes have similar annual costs, but they have to be paid for a lifetime.

As we went through the tour, I remember my spirits lifted tremendously. There were no tears, and I found myself actually feeling a little smug. I had to admit the homes were very nice, and although they did not have too many people who required one-on-one caregiving like my brother, the option was available.

However, as I walked around, I remembered what people told me about visiting colleges: "You will know the right one as soon as you step foot on campus." Walking around the Pathfinder Village, I did not have this kind of feeling, so I just assumed it must not be the right place for Robb. Besides, it was in upstate New York, and we lived in Maryland. It was cold. They did not have a pool on site. I made a list in my head of all the features I hoped to see at the next place we visited, and I smiled when I thought about visiting even better places for Robb that were closer to home. People had spoken very highly of this place, but I knew that it could not possibly be the right option for Robb.

As the tour concluded and our guide walked away, I expected to turn around and laugh with my dad about how lucky we were this was not the perfect place. In my mind, the decision became easier: Robb would stay in Maryland because the homes there must be just as good for him as those at Pathfinder.

However, when the guide was out of earshot, my dad started talking about how this was the best place he had ever seen. He mentioned he was not surprised as everyone had told him it was one of only a few places like it in the country. He called my mom and told her how amazing it was. He said she would have broken down in tears if she had been on the tour.

At first I felt sadness, but the feeling quickly turned to anger as I realized the difference between looking at colleges and looking at housing for people with IDD: I could search for my perfect or near-perfect college, but for Robb, we were just looking to see if there was even an option that was adequate. Furthermore, once we found that place, we would need to get on a miles-long waiting list until there was a space for him.

Throughout my life, I was always aware of the stigma and misconceptions surrounding the population of people with IDD.

Oftentimes, my family has been pitied as if Robb were a burden rather than a human being deserving of love and support. My parents received consolation cards when Robb was born. Once, after Robb came and sat down by a peer and me when we were ten, the girl turned to my mom and asked, "Does Robb get happy and sad like *a real person*?" We even went to a dinner party where the hostess forgot to set a place for my brother.

Despite my understanding of the prejudice toward the community of people with IDD, in that moment, I was shocked at my own lack of knowledge about the IDD housing crisis that would directly affect my brother.

**

The only time I had ever thought about what my brother would do after high school before the Pathfinder tour was when I attended Special Olympics practice with a friend who was really interested in seeing the program. We were waiting for Robb to finish changing so we could leave, and I was explaining to him the wide age range of athletes on our team—Our oldest athlete being around 60 at the time. When

I mentioned the large number of adult athletes involved in the program as they walked out of the facility, my friend asked me, "Where do they go?" What he was really asking was, "Where do they live? What happens to them when they are not at Special Olympics? What are they doing 99% of the time?" I mulled over the question, and the only thing that came to mind was a phrase I had occasionally heard: "assisted living." Then, with all the confidence of a self-proclaimed thirteen-year-old expert, I said, "Many people with special needs have assisted living." And that was that. I didn't even know what assisted living meant, but it was a phrase I could use to eliminate worry and thought on my part about Robb's future.

**

Some people may read this and wonder why Robb would not just live with my parents as an adult, and this is certainly an option. Over 70% of adults with IDD, as of 2015, reported living with their parents or guardian.[7] However, this option is only viable for so long. Adults with IDD cannot be cared for by their aging parents forever, and because of this temporary solution, many aging caregivers don't have a plan for what

---

7 Braddock, David, Nicole T. Jorwic, Amie Lulinski, and Emily Shea Tanis. "Rebalancing of Long-Term Supports and Services for Individuals with Intellectual and Developmental Disabilities in the United States." *The State of the States in Intellectual and Developmental Disabilities Data Brief 2018*, 2018.

will happen to their adult children when they themselves can no longer care for them.

I decided to begin looking into group housing options throughout the country so that I could truly understood my brother's options, and how I could help make his experience as an adult as positive as possible. I know firsthand what it feels like to a family member going through the housing process, and after writing this book, while I am far from being the expert I once claimed to be, I know how important it is to spread the word about the positive techniques which are available.

This book focuses on group homes (with a couple exceptions) because they are the largest provider of homes for adults with IDD.[8] Although state definitions of group homes for people with disabilities differ, the definition used in this book refers to homes with no more than six people where unrelated individuals with IDD live and receive services. (Note: Some housing options falling under the same definition I have just shared reject the term "group home." The nomenclature used in the following chapters will correspond with the preferences of the organization being discussed.)

---

8   Ibid.

While there are international organizations that operate group homes, *Ability Innovation* touches on group homes in the United States to ensure the techniques being used are in compliance with federal law. Also, if advocates push to enact the systems discussed in their state, they have a tried and true example of the technique's success.

**

I wrote this book because I wanted to share who is doing what to establish more quality housing opportunities for adults with IDD and how some of these changes are being and can be implemented in group homes nationwide. I'm happy to report there are lots of people finding innovative ways to address the housing and caregiving needs of this population. More is needed, to be sure, but there are many examples of incredible people doing wonderful things to help adults with IDD get housing and support. It is my pleasure to describe many of them to you throughout the pages of this book.

First and foremost, this book is a tool for parents and siblings of people with IDD and professionals in the disability housing field alike who want to explore innovations which they can then use to elevate the quality of group housing options. However, I hope that anyone with an entrepreneurial spirit can use this book as a roadmap to developing their own housing solution. I do not want to sugarcoat the fact that we are currently on the brink of crisis as more and more people do not have access to quality housing options. However, only when people can see the opportunity in the face of crisis can there be real change.

**

The Centre for Applied Disability Research (CADR) in Australia identifies four key aspects of group homes: physical design, culture, practice of the staff, and policies/procedures.[9] Upon starting this book, I kept these different categories in mind as I explored the efforts of those who were creating new and innovative solutions in housing for people with IDD. However, as I continued my research, I decided to focus on innovation in the following categories: finding group homes, home design, staff/resident relationship, and community relations. And although I do not address the topic directly due to all of the nuances based on state, funding and financing is still a recurring subject in all such efforts. However, the key overarching theme is even more basic than any of these:

Empathy.

---

9   Bigby, C. and E. Bould. "Guide to Good Group Homes, Evidence about what makes the most difference to the quality of group homes." 2017. *Centre for Applied Disability Research.*

It is only through empathy and understanding a person before their disability, that the right kinds of programs and opportunities can be established to serve the needs of adults with IDD.

HOW TO READ
THIS BOOK

———

FOR A FAMILY MEMBER

First, answer the question: Where is your family in the housing process? We are currently looking for a housing option for my brother, so Pathways to a Home would be the most helpful place for my family to start. This chapter may be largely superfluous (albeit interesting!) for individuals who already have housing arrangements.

Communicate with your son/daughter/brother/sister/ cousin/etc. who will be living in the home! These are the people who will be affected most by the housing choice and changes to practices in their home. What do they consider crucial for a positive housing experience?

If your loved one is already in a group home, think about areas for improvement. Do you or your loved one feel like there is not enough technology being utilized in the home? Do you all struggle with the staff in the home? Have you all felt isolated from the community? If you answered yes to any of the questions above, turn to the section which addresses innovations in these areas. While some chapters will highlight large-scale models, there will always be examples of smaller-scale improvements which can be made.

Use the section introductions. Unsure what chapters will provide information most relevant to your needs? The section introductions were created to give you a roadmap to the chapters within. From there, you can decide what information will be the most useful for your loved one.

FOR POLICY MAKERS AND GROUP HOME AGENCIES

Read it. Know it. Explore. When you are determining the fates of different housing options, you need to understand what is out there. This book covers only a sliver of all of the different housing options and new innovations in the field, so use it as a starting point in your journey to learn about the new approaches being taken and appreciate the value of variety in housing. The more practices you know, the more avenues to a solution you can find.

FOR A BUDDING ENTREPRENEUR, INTERESTED IN THE IDD HOUSING FIELD

Look for Sections that Interest YOU and Dive Right In! All of the people with whom I've spoken had one thing in common: passion. To be successful in this field, you have to be passionate about the work you are doing.

Connect. This book provides information about all of the organizations discussed. If you want to emulate something they have done, reach out! We are all working toward a common goal of making the best experience possible for people in the IDD community.

FOR ANYONE NEW TO THE DISABILITY COMMUNITY

Welcome!

Skip Liberally. This is not just a book of information, but it is a collection of stories about people connected to the IDD community, as well as their triumphs and struggles. Read the stories that interest you so you can really empathize with the people within.

Notice Vocabulary. While all organizations use different vocabulary to describe their services, pay attention to overarching trends. Language surrounding disability and disability housing continues to evolve, but one key element is to use person-first language and put people before their disability. (For example, instead of "disabled person," say "person with a disability.")

Start the Conversation. The only way we can help to end the housing crisis is by spreading awareness about the issue and the solutions.

CHAPTER 1:

EVOLUTION FROM INSTITUTIONALIZATION TO GROUP HOUSING

———

Note: In this book, I use the widely-recognized term "intellectual and developmental disabilities" (IDD). Although individuals in the following chapter use the words "insane," "retard," "idiot," and "feeble-minded" to refer to individuals living with IDD, these are no longer acceptable ways to refer to people in this population. The use of such language is both derogatory and pejorative.

INSTITUTIONALIZATION IN THE NINETEENTH CENTURY

In the first British colonies established in what would eventually become the United States of America, it was seen as each town's responsibility to care for individuals with intellectual and developmental disabilities. For wealthy families, these individuals could live in the family home, but for others, it often meant being sent to "almshouses," facilities operated by local governments which housed people with disabilities, impoverished individuals, and criminals.

By the time Dorothea Dix began observing Massachusetts almshouses in 1840, they had grown from being scattered around in various towns to being present in nearly every town and city. Some were small houses consisting of only ten or twelve residents while others had as many as one thousand individuals, but they all had the same goal: confining individuals with IDD and keeping them separate from a society in which they were considered burdens.

After Dix's comprehensive assessment of almshouses throughout Massachusetts, she presented her findings to the state legislature in *A Memorial to the Massachusetts Legislature* (1843), in which she noted the following:

> I proceed, gentlemen, briefly to call your attention to the present state of insane persons confined within

this Commonwealth, in cages, closets, cellars, stalls, pens! Chained, naked, beaten with rods, and lashed into obedience.[10]

Dix didn't hold anything back as she described what she observed during her visits to the almshouses of Massachusetts:

Lincoln. A woman in a cage. Medford. One idiotic subject chained, and one in a close stall for seventeen years. Pepperell. One often doubly chained, hand and foot; another violent; several peaceable now. Brookfield. One man caged, comfortable. Granville. One often closely confined; now losing the use of his limbs from want of exercise. Charlemont. One man caged. Savoy. One man caged. Lenox. Two in the jail, against whose unfit condition there the jailer protests.[11]

She continued to make observations and conduct her assessments in other states, despite her poor health and struggles with depression. She expanded her campaign to New York, New Jersey, Pennsylvania, Maryland, Ohio, Kentucky, and Tennessee. On April 10, 1844, *Providence Journal* published an article she wrote titled "Astonishing Tenacity of Life." She described how Abram Simmons, a man with severe

---

10   Dix, Dorothea. "The History of Mental Retardation, Collected Papers." *University Parks Press.*,1843.

11   Ibid.

intellectual disabilities who she had visited in a Rhode Island jail, was being held in a stone cell enclosed by two iron doors. He was in complete darkness without any fresh air. All of the walls were covered in frost, and due to a leaky roof, the straw bed and the man's clothes were all wet. Dix exclaimed, "His teeth must have been worn out by constant and violent chattering for such a length of time, night and day."[12]

What Dorothea Dix accomplished in a relatively short amount of time was nothing short of amazing. By 1845, Dix had traveled throughout the midwest and south to visit eighteen state penitentiaries, three hundred county jails, and over five hundred poorhouses. During this time, she advocated for legislation protecting people with IDD, and she helped create six new hospitals for people with IDD in addition to improving existing facilities.

The more she traveled and the more she saw how people with IDD were being treated, Dix realized that what was really needed were serious changes and reforms at the federal level. She wanted to present one of her "memorials" to Congress, but in those days, a woman directly addressing the nation's legislative body was out of the question. She enlisted the help of well-known social reformer, Dr. Samuel Gridley Howe, who presented her speech for her. Once again, Dix

12   Dix, Dorothea. "Astonishing Tenacity of Life." Providence Journal, April 10, 1844..

laid out the bare truth of what was happening throughout the country:

> More than nine-thousand idiots, epileptics, and insane in these United States, destitute of appropriate care and protection. Bound with galling chains, bowed beneath fetters and heavy iron balls, attached to drag-chains, lacerated with ropes, scourged with rods, and terrified beneath storms of profane execrations and cruel blows; now subject to jibes, and scorn, and torturing tricks, now abandoned to the most loathsome necessities or subject to the vilest and most outrageous violations.[13]

Dix advocated that instead of lumping people with IDD in with other different groups (primarily homeless people and criminals), there should be places focusing solely on improving the situations of people with IDD. Her appeal to Congress was to use federal funds to create places where people could live quality lives, receiving the proper care and support they deserved. Her requests were denied several times before a bill was finally passed by both houses of Congress in 1854. Unfortunately, it was then vetoed by President Franklin Pierce, who was reticent to expand the federal government's authority into areas he considered best left to state and local

---

13   "Make the Deviant Undeviant." *Parallels In Time: A History of Developmental Disabilities.*

governments. In those days, there was no federal income tax, and Pierce didn't want the federal government to become responsible for all the "indigent insane" throughout the country.[14]

Meanwhile, Dr. Howe had been researching how to handle the education of people with IDD. In 1848, he opened the first Massachusetts School for Idiotic and Feeble-Minded Youth. Both he and Dix advocated not just for better facilities for these individuals, but also the idea that people with IDD could learn and grow, and even be well-integrated in society instead of being segregated. The school was a success, and more began opening throughout the country.

However, as schools continued to open, their purpose began shifting away from educational goals. Because of the influx of immigrants after the Civil War, many people with IDD who returned to their communities after gaining an education could not get jobs. Also, during the recession of the 1870s, these schools became underfunded, and government officials focused on economic recovery over the moral imperative to serve this population. The number of people enrolled in these schools kept growing, but the lack of resources ended up turning them into little more than holding tanks for the residents. The higher-functioning individuals who did

---

14   Warder, Graham. "Franklin Pierce's 1854 Veto." *Disability History Museum.*

receive an education often ended up applying it only within the confines of the institutions themselves.

When Howe was asked to give a keynote speech at an institution being developed in Batvia, New York, he warned, "We should be cautious about such artificial communities, or those approaching them in character, for any children and youth; but more especially should we avoid them for those who have natural infirmities, or any marked peculiarity of mental organization ... The home of the blind and of the mutes should be his native town or village; there, if possible, he should live during childhood and youth; there he should form his friendships; there, if he comes to need special aid, it will be given most readily and fitly; and there his old age will be cherished."[15] Although Howe could see how his original educational vision for all people with disabilities was devolving into what we now call "institutionalization," he was powerless to stop it. As a result, people living with IDD once again faced neglect and abuse.

TURN OF THE CENTURY EUGENICS AND SEGREGATION

Along with the influx of immigrants displacing individuals with IDD from jobs, the emergence of the eugenics

---

15 "Howe's Speech In Batavia." *Disability History.*

movement further solidified the belief that people with IDD needed to be segregated from society. People thought societal improvement could only be attained by separating and even eliminating populations of people who could not contribute in the same ways as others.[16] Alexander Johnson, President of the National Conference on Charities and Corrections during the late nineteenth century, advocated for keeping "defectives" away from society and ensuring they could not have children. In the March 1906 edition of the *Journal of Psycho-Asthenics*, Johnson describes what he thinks is the right way to respond to a family with a child exhibiting developmental disabilities: "… in all probability, the child will never develop so it is wise and to the best interests of the child, of the family or of society, never to discharge him from your institution."[17] Toward the end of the same article, Johnson quotes from a report by Mary E. Perry:… we are able to put a stop to the fast increasing population of the epileptic and feeble-minded. I believe the remedy is largely in the hands of this conference and instead of reporting annually the statistics and the facts about these people, it would now be well to prepare our several states to call to their assistance the surgeon's knife to

---

16 Grenon, Ingrid, and Joav Merrick. "Intellectual And Developmental Disabilities: Eugenics". October 20, 2014. Frontiers In Public Health 2. Frontiers Media SA. doi:10.3389/fpubh.2014.00201.

17 Johnson, A. "The Segregation And Permanent Detention Of The Feeble-Minded." Journal of *Psycho-Asthenics,* March, 1906.

prevent the entailing of this curse upon innocent numbers of yet unborn children.[18]

Make no mistake, Johnson was advocating for the forced sterilization of people with IDD, and twenty-one years later in the Supreme Court case Buck v. Bell, 274 U.S. 200 (1927), the justices ruled in favor of forced sterilization of individuals with IDD, thereby stripping them of their autonomy.[19]

Despite Dr. Howe's earlier research, which disproved Johnson's claims that people with IDD could not be educated, Johnson's arguments in favor of institutionalization would hold sway for many decades onward. In 1883, Massachusetts Governor Benjamin Butler verbalized the feelings of many that the disabled were neither deserving or capable of benefitting from education, stating: "Give them an asylum, with good and kind treatment; but not a school" and "A well-fed, well-cared for idiot, is a happy creature. An idiot awakened to his condition is a miserable one."[20] As Howe's schools transformed into institutionalized holding-tanks, people began to take on vocabulary and frameworks of thought similar to what is used for prisons, which historian David

---

18 Ibid.
19 "Buck vs. Bell Trial." *Eugenics Archive.*
20 Wolfensberger, Wolf. 'Changing Patterns in Residential Services for the Mentally Retarded." *President's Committee on Mental Retardation,* Washington, D.C. January 10, 1969.

Vail dubbed the "dehumanizing process."[21] The "pupils" became "inmates," and even in census reports, the number of people with disabilities was reported alongside social problems of the time such as crime and prostitution. One textbook published in the early twentieth century, "The Almosts: A Study of the Feeble-Minded" even described people with IDD as only "almost human."[22]

These institutional asylums continued to grow throughout the first five decades of the twentieth century, and oftentimes were the only options available to parents of children with IDD. Doctors would tell them that upon the birth of their child, they had to look into institutions because it was the best option even though the norms in those institutions were likely to include overcrowding and mistreatment. Living in an institution often meant staying in one large room for the entire day with no stimulating activities. People who were higher-functioning became unpaid labor, and individuals who were considered difficult to control would be tied to beds or restrained with straitjackets. As punishment, guards would also beat individuals into submission. These conditions were comparable to what Dorothea Dix had described and campaigned against over a century before.

---

21 "From Training School to Asylum." *Parallels In Time: A History of Developmental Disabilities.*

22 "History Context–Leadership in the History of the Developmental Disabilities Movement." *Disability History.*

The segregation and attempt to completely remove individuals with IDD from society was poignant in parents' reactions to their children. Parents would often hide the fact that their child was born with IDD because people often believed the parents were somehow at fault for causing the child's disability. When Phil Roos, a professional who diagnosed IDD in children, found out his own child had IDD, he lost credibility in his profession: "I had suddenly been demoted from the role of a professional to that of the parent as patient; the assumption by some professionals that parents of a retarded child are emotionally maladjusted."[23]

REVOLUTION AND DEINSTITUTIONALIZATION

It wasn't until the 1950s when two famous individuals emerged and spoke out against stigmatizing people with disabilities that perceptions began to change. One was Pearl Buck, winner of both the Pulitzer and Nobel Prizes, who published a book about her child with IDD titled "The Child Who Never Grew." The other was Dale Evans Rogers, a television and movie star at the time, who told the public about her daughter with Down Syndrome who had died at the age of two. These parents, along with countless others who followed suit, became part of a growing movement calling for increased advocacy and change. However, even as the blame

---

23 "Reasons Why Parents Organized." *Parallels In Time: A History of Developmental Disabilities.*

placed on parents softened, children being born with IDD during the post-war baby-boom were still largely seen as burdens to their families, and institutionalization was still advised.[24]

Another major catalyst for change came when John F. Kennedy became president of the United States. Because his sister Rosemary had lived with a developmental disability, Kennedy's family could empathize with the horrible conditions to which people in these institutions were subject. The Kennedy family became dedicated to improving (although not eliminating) the systems in place.

In 1961, JFK launched the first "President's Panel on Mental Retardation" dedicated to improving conditions for individuals with IDD, and in 1963 he signed the Community Mental Health Act into law, the goal of which was to reduce the number of people in institutions by 50 percent.[25]

In 1965, JFK's brother Robert Kennedy was a senator for the state of New York. He made an unannounced visit to a state asylum called Willowbrook State School and spoke out about the horrors he saw there:I think that at the state institution

---

24 "1950 – 1970 Improve the Institutions." *Parallels In Time: A History of Developmental Disabilities.*

25 "1947 – 1980 The Parents' Movement." *Parallels In Time: A History of Developmental Disabilities.*

for the mentally retarded, and I think that particularly at Willowbrook, we have a situation that borders on a snake pit, and that the children live in filth, that many of our fellow citizens are suffering tremendously because of lack of attention, lack of imagination, lack of adequate manpower. There is very little future for these children, for those who are in these institutions. Both need a tremendous overhauling. I'm not saying that those who are the attendants there, or who run the institutions, are at fault – I think all of us are at fault and I think it's just long overdue that something be done about it.[26]

Although more citizens were becoming aware of the problem, actual change was still slow in coming. Seven years after Robert Kennedy's visit to Willowbrook, a young reporter named Geraldo Rivera visited in 1972 and created a twenty-eight-minute news report revealing the truly nightmarish conditions.[27] Every television network picked up the story and ran with it. The nation was shocked at what Rivera depicted in his short documentary, *Willowbrook: The Last Great Disgrace.*[28] There was national outrage when Rivera's

26 "Best Practices in Supported Employment." *Agency for Persons with Disabilities (State of Florida),* January 1, 2015.

27 Brown, Dalton. "The Horrifying Truth Uncovered: Willowbrook State School." *Rooted In Rights,* October 15, 2014.

28 Primo, Albert T., Executive Producer. *Willowbrook: The Last Great Disgrace,* 1972. SproutFlix.

exposé hit the airwaves, and the trend of increased awareness continued throughout the rest of the twentieth century.

In 1978, the National Council on Disabilities was first created within the Department of Education to examine strategies for increased disability inclusion, and less than a decade later, in 1984, the council became an independent agency which reviewed all disability policy.[29] In 1986, the council released a study titled *Towards Independence,* which stated that the main barrier preventing increased independence for people with disabilities was the continued violation of the rights of people with disabilities. This report prompted the creation of the Americans with Disabilities Act in 1990 with the main goal of eliminating all discrimination of people with disabilities including in the housing sector.[30]

This legislation provided a base for rapid change in disability treatment most exemplified, with regard to housing, by two women with IDD living in Georgia. Lois Curtis and Elaine Wilson both struggled as they moved in and out of state institutions. After living in the hospitals, they moved back to their community in the hopes of living more independent lives, but without the appropriate supports, they had to return to the hospital. The doctors were clear that if they

---

29 "About Us." *National Council on Disability.*
30 "ADA – Findings, Purpose, and History." *ADA 30.*

just had the right supports, they could achieve independent housing. Curtis and Wilson, with the help of Atlanta Legal Aid attorney Susan Jamieson, sued the state of Georgia for not providing integrated services.[31]

The case reached the Supreme Court who ruled in favor of the women. The high court determined the state was violating the Americans with Disabilities Act by limiting their housing options based on their disabilities. This ruling in 1999, which is now referred to as the Olmstead Decision, was the first legal precedent set against the unnecessary segregation of people with disabilities and in favor of requiring people with IDD to be given access to community living options. Justice Ruth Bader Ginsberg announced the court's decision:

> She stated that the Supreme Court answered with a "qualified yes" the question of whether the ADA's prohibition of discrimination by a public entity required "placement of persons with mental disabilities in community settings rather than in institutions." The Supreme Court created three requirements for when such action is required: (1) when treatment professionals determine that community placement is appropriate; (2) when the individual does not oppose being served in the community; and (3)

---

31 "Unlocked: The Lois Curtis Story." *Robin Rayne: A Souther Photojournalist's Notebook,* November 27, 2010.

when the placement is a reasonable accommodation when balanced with the needs of others with mental disabilities.[32]

From around 200,000 people in institutions at their peak in 1967, the number of people in state-run institutions fell to under 35,000 in 2009, and it continues to decrease. Likewise, the number of community-based living centers have continued to increase, and the centers strive to make the community of people with disabilities one that is actually a part of the wider community.[33] Specifically, group homes have become the most common form of housing for individuals with IDD who are not living in the homes of their families, and the states have begun to focus on supporting individuals on a case-by-case basis, recognizing not every living situation is right for everyone. However, there is still a long way to go for IDD housing in terms of availability and affordability.

When my parents went to the court to request guardianship for my brother, they met another family who had gone through a similar process, and my father got to talk to them about where we were in the process of preparing for adulthood. My brother was 18, which meant he could only be a part of the public school system for three more years. In

32 "Olmstead v. LC: History and Current Status." *Olmstead Rights.*
33 "Institutions in Brief." *National Council on Disability,* 2012.

the meantime, my family was trying to do everything we could to make sure there was something in place after he graduated. My house was always filled with stacks of books and pamphlets and hundred-page forms for applying for services, whether it was caregiver hours or financial assistance.I remember reading the forms where my parents had to describe all of the worst parts of my brother, such as how he hit his head when he was angry or how he chewed his finger and caused infections. Once while walking into the kitchen, I glimpsed the negative review of my brother on the form, and I confronted my mom. How she could focus on his challenges rather than his strengths? It was then that I learned all the empowerment and enlightenment in the world would not get Robb the supports he needed. It felt to me like the Developmental Disability Administration was looking not to support humans, but to limit the financial burdens it was taking on.

However, my dad did not need to tell the couple standing in front of him about the process of finding support, and when my dad mentioned my brother's looming 21st birthday, they simply replied, "You mean when they push you off the cliff." They meant the disability cliff—when children with IDD become adults and are no longer entitled to schooling or anything in the ways of special services.

We have come a long way from forced institutionalization, but we are still only at the very early stages of the long journey to optimizing the IDD housing system and ensuring that there are enough resources available for individuals with IDD to live rich, fulfilling lives. However, as we shift into the present, and more specifically as we begin to examine the pathways towards finding suitable housing options, we must continually look to history to ensure the mistakes of the past are not repeated as we work hard to create a brighter future for adults with IDD.

PATHWAYS
TO A HOME
INTRODUCTION

Now that we have finished our journey through time, we will begin looking at the pathways to a home. For my family, this path started when my brother was 16, five years before he would even be able to move out of my parents' house. For most families, the individual with IDD has reached adulthood before the path begins. And unfortunately for many parents, they wait to begin the journey until it is too late. Starting on this path is the most important step for families to ensure that their loved one finds a living situation right for them. We can only improve someone's living situation if they have a place to live to begin with.

This section examines organizations which have created new approaches to helping people transition into a housing option. The first two chapters will focus on two different pathways to housing: looking for an option which already exists or developing your own housing option and forging your own path respectively. The organizations discussed are working to improve everyone's pathway to a home on a national scale.

The third and final chapter of Pathways to a Home will discuss the key to positive housing outcomes:

Choice.

Just as all paths to a home will be different, every individual will have a unique housing option that works for them. While this book focuses on group homes, these will not be the right option for everyone. Furthermore, as we will see throughout this book, every group home will be different to fit the needs and lifestyles of the residents.

CHAPTER 2:

FINDING A HOME

———

Because institutional settings have largely dissolved and been replaced by many smaller homes located throughout the community, the question arises as to how to find the homes that are available and determine the right option. The process is daunting, and oftentimes, families must spend vast amounts of time to find the right place. My parents began looking for housing options when my brother was 16, and over the past three years, planning my brother's future has become my mom's full-time job.

First comes finding the organizations. Every family is entitled to a service coordinator (though many people do not realize they need one). The service coordinator helps families apply for financial support through the Developmental Disabilities Administration (DDA) and connects them to services in the state.[34] This individual has given my parents lists of certain housing options. Also, the Maryland DDA provides a list of housing options on their website.[35] However, both resources are *lists*: just names of organizations on a piece of paper or website without any in-depth information.

Also, oftentimes when speaking to other parents, my mom hears about organizations that are not listed on either of these two resources. Therefore, contacting other parents and meeting with them has also become another path my mom takes to find options.

After finding out about an organization, the next step is usually looking at the websites. Unfortunately, many organizations' websites prove relatively useless as they provide little to no information on even the most basic facts (level of care provided, availability, etc.). The lack of information online has required my mother to visit every possible location in person, and she often tries to speak to residents and families of residents as well. In some cases, my mom will be on a tour before discovering the organization does not even provide the level of service Robb needs.

---

34 "Your Service Coordinator." *Service Coordination.*
35 "Family Supports Waiver Providers." *Maryland Department of Health Developmental Disabilities Administration,* January 4, 2019.

So far, she has visited over forty agencies along with other homes run by families themselves throughout the state (and two farmsteads in Kentucky and Pennsylvania). Most of these places have been at least an hour from our house. She always says that "as a parent when you hear of any possible opportunity you have to go see it," but even after all of the places she has seen, we still have no idea where Robb will live as an adult.

While finding the right living situation for someone's adult life will always take time, the scattered and scanty information vastly increases the time required to find a housing option. Autism Housing Network is trying to localize the options for shared living and other types of adult housing into one database to make the process a little less daunting. (The moment I shared it with my mom, she signed up for an account!)

AUTISM HOUSING NETWORK

Desiree Kameka, founder of the Autism Housing Network (AHN), left seminary school in 2009 knowing she wanted a career in the disability field: "I fell in love with this population in high school volunteering at a YMCA special needs camp and when I went to undergraduate, I worked for the Center for Autism and Related Disabilities." However, it was only when she got in contact with the seminary admissions office about jobs relating to autism that she met JaLynn Prince.JaLynn Prince is the founder and president of Madison House Autism Foundation, an organization created to focus on and address the challenges faced by adults with autism. When she hired Desiree as a research intern, Jalynn asked her, "Can you find the holes in autism in adulthood? What is not being worked on by other organizations?" Neither of them realized it then, but Desiree's work with Madison House would make her and the organization a trailblazer in housing accessibility nationwide.

Because Desiree had only worked with kids and teenagers on the spectrum, her first realization in her research was about how many "holes" there were in supports for adults with autism and other disabilities: "When I would ask their parents what was happening after graduation, their parents were really concerned, and I had not realized that beforehand."

She then went on to pinpoint exactly from where the concerns stemmed, and upon looking at larger organizations: "I saw a lot of things on first responders, on employment, but I really didn't see anyone talking about housing," she said. Desiree continued to look into housing and the potential in that market: "If we spend all this time and energy looking at employment and day programming and building a natural support system, but someone's forced to leave their community then we've lost all of that effort."

When deciding how to address the problems with housing, access to information became an increasingly important issue. She spoke with self-advocates, families, housing organizations, policy makers, and other people in the disability field nationwide and came to a realization:

> People have to just put things into a Google search and hope for the best, so I thought it would be really important that there was a central database where people could add resources that are applicable and that are helpful. Also, a place where people can access lots of different resources that are all related to housing and lifespan issues.

Within the first couple months of her research at the Madison House Autism Foundation, Desiree began developing the plan for the Autism Housing Network, and she now serves as the director for the service. The Autism Housing Network has multiple functions, but Desiree's overarching goal is "to bring together partnerships in local communities." Her directory includes a database of housing options for adults with intellectual disabilities (not limited to autism) throughout the country, and in addition to shared living (another term for group homes), she includes farmsteads, single apartments, and more.

Also, there are various filters so that people can tailor their search to their loved one's specific needs. The filters for the homes include quantitative information like payment options, support levels, and availability along with information based on social preferences. For example, families can filter the results based on features of the home including if they allow pets or have sensory-friendly design. Another filter is "primary residents," in which people can decide whether they are looking for solely residents with disabilities or a neurodiverse community where people with and without disabilities live together.

Even though the database is monitored by Desiree and other employees of the Madison House Autism Foundation and she often invites organizations to join AHN, Desiree does not add any organizations to the database herself:

> Someone from the organization or a parent or a self advocate, they need to fill out the form to add a listing because I want it to be in the nomenclature and the rhetoric of the organization ... that tells a little bit about who they are and about their culture.

The network also includes resources for gaining supports and services in the process of developing a housing plan which are written both by AHN employees as well as advocates throughout the country. These resources can be filtered based on individual questions and concerns. In addition, the website includes a discussion module where individuals can connect with others in similar situations or experts to have an open dialogue about the housing process and their specific concerns. Desiree Kameka herself is an active participant on the discussion board, and she is always ready to help people with questions about the process.

When describing the database, Desiree focuses not just on the resources they provide, but what families can share with each other, "The AHN is the first interactive online community for adults with special needs and their families." Although the process requires a time investment, if one family could speak to others who have been through the process in their area, they can get advice about how to spend their time effectively.

On the homepage of the AHN, the organization shares a horrifying statistic: Only one in ten individuals with IDD have enough available resources to allow them to move into their own home. However, every day this organization works to eliminate the barrier between the resources and those who need them. Even though at the time of this writing in 2019, the database is still in BETA mode, it includes over 125 differ-ent housing options from throughout the country and over 250 resources for people looking for housing or looking to develop housing, and it continues to grow daily. "We believe that our community has the power to change the future of housing for adults with autism and other IDD."

CHAPTER 3:

CREATING A HOME

Although AHN is doing exciting work to help people find a housing option that's right for them, the options that are available now cannot meet the growing need nationwide.

This fact became strikingly clear to me after visiting a group home and day service provider in Carroll County with my mom in the spring of 2019. We were shown around the facility, introduced to individuals working at the company, and given a chance to ask questions about the homes. They have a truly fantastic model which will continue to come up in following chapters. However, when it came to the Q&A at the end of our tour, it became clear that this option would not be feasible for my brother. Here is my paraphrased memory of our conversation with an employee:

We had just entered the room, and my mom could not help but exclaim, "This program is just so amazing! I guess the only question we have left is about the application process."

The employee replied, "Well, when people with IDD in Carrol County are aging out of the school system, we actually track them and work with other organizations in the area to try and help them find potential housing options. That way we can make sure that everyone in the county has an option available when they graduate, and the transition is as seamless as possible."

This sounds really great for people in Carroll County, and we weren't surprised. This county is known for providing the best services in Maryland to its residents with IDD. Except we don't live in Carroll County. Both my mom and I began to squirm a little in our seats, and trying to clarify as politely as possible, my mom replied, "So how many applicants do you have from areas outside of Carroll County?"

The woman gave us a blank look. "Because we are a small program, we often cannot even take all of the applicants who want to enter our homes from Carroll County, and we still have people on our wait-list who live within Carroll County," she said.

The hope in this option for my brother slowly began to dwindle. Up until this point, we knew that Robb's funding could not travel outside of Maryland, but we had not considered that housing options might be limited to our county. We blinked at each other for a little while before my mom replied, "Is it possible to enter into your home from outside of Carroll County?" "In some circumstances, yes, but you have to understand we have people who are waiting to get into our program for years who live within the county, and we will serve those people first."

After she finished speaking, it was about the perfect time for a cricket chirp. She had now mentioned the importance of living in Carroll County three times and the difficulty of getting into the program twice. When the meeting ended a few minutes later, and we got into the car to drive home, the only logical conversation topic that came to mind was how soon we could sell our house and move to Carroll County.

This story of "we just don't have space" has become a constant for my family and many others because most housing options do not have an opening until one of their residents dies. Waitlists are miles long. As of 2010, 115,089 Medicaid-eligible people with IDD were on waiting lists for residential services, and the number has only continued to increase over the past decade.[36] However, due to the lack of space, more and more families are looking at how to use government funding and personal resources to piece together and create an optimal home for their adult child.

Autism Housing Network does provide information about the best practices for developing housing. As Desiree explains, "It serves as a hub of housing ideas and resources to help project-starters create new options for thousands of adults with autism and related disabilities across the nation." However, the two innovative approaches described below have both developed new processes to help families create group living. Center for Independent Futures helps parents in Evanston, Illinois, through the process of finding housing and work opportunities, and it also provides intensive workshops to parents worldwide about how to develop and manage housing in their community. Partners4Housing has developed a roommate matching service for individuals with IDD and provides consulting to help families through the process of developing a home.

CENTER FOR INDEPENDENT FUTURES

"He just knows a tremendous amount of stuff." When people meet Jonathan, they are always amazed by his wealth of

---

36 "Our Model." *LTO Ventures.*

information. Whether it is that his birthday is the same day that Julius Caesar was killed or a review to a movie he has recently seen, he not only retains but is ready to share the information with his friends, co-workers, and roommate. However, Jonathan's parents did not always know that the future would allow him to have so many people with whom he could share his thoughts. His mom, Joelle Gabay, explains that many of her worries were about adult life: "There is this big anxiety about the future: he will never have a job, he will never have a friend." Jonathan's family is not the only one to experience these fears. As his father, Howard Shuman explains,

> Anytime a parent has a child with special needs, you are kind of instantaneously immersed in this different world for which you have no background or training or anything, and you sort of have to figure it out as you go along.

When Jonathan was about to graduate high school and his family began looking for the right program, they found the Center for Independent Futures located where they lived in Evanston, Illinois, a suburb of Chicago. As explained by Executive Director, Ann Sickon, "Center for Independent Futures is there to really help individuals with disabilities and their families create new options, new solutions." Rather than focusing on one aspect of the move to adulthood, they tackle different facets to help individuals build a life. With Jonathan, the group has successfully helped connect him with an employer where he works, given him weekly tutoring focusing on different life skills, and found him a home and a roommate, along with a caregiver.[37]

In the housing field, the organization's New Futures Initiative is truly exceptional. It is a step-by-step process in which Center for Independent Futures takes families through a series of workshops to help them determine every aspect of the living arrangement for their loved one. The system was developed both by family members who have gone through the process and leaders in the field of community development, and the system has worked for hundreds of families.[38]

Although Jonathan's family was based in Evanston, which meant they could work with the company directly, families nationwide can go in for workshops to get an intensive course on how they can manage housing and other services required for their loved one to live independently.

Bill Godfrey, the executive director of Three Oaks, an intentional community building service, has even used the company to help prepare families when they enter intentional

37 *Living a Full Life: Jonathan's Story.* Center for Independent Futures, April 27, 2015.
38 "Creating Housing Options." *Center for Independent Futures.*

communities developed by him. "They've got a really great model, so what we decided to do is have all of the families of our IDD home buyers go to Chicago for a three-day training." Bill considers this training so crucial to the success of developing plans for adults with IDD, that for any families going to the program, they will underwrite the costs of the training.

When Jonathan was first born, his parents did not think he would be able to be independent, but now Jonathan cannot picture his life any other way. When talking about the program to others, Jonathan said, "It feels great to be independent because I get to make my own choices. I get to make my own decisions."

When his parents looked back on the process, they felt that having the organization walking them through it was crucial to their success:

> Jonathan is close to having achieved a lot of his potential: living very independently, taking transportation, having friends, and having a job. I think this is something that you can't create yourself. You have to have this wonderful organization, Center for Independent Futures to help you do that.[39]

---

39 *Living a Full Life: Jonathan's Story.* Center for Independent Futures, April 27, 2015.

PARTNERS4HOUSING

The advice on how to develop and run a community living option provided by Center for Independent Futures is also a service Partners4Housing offers. Partners4Housing is a consulting business based in Seattle, Washington, that helps people create a housing solution to meet the unique needs of their loved one with a disability. Moreover, this organization has revolutionized how people find roommates through their online roommate matching service.

Pam Blanton was no stranger to the problems of housing for people with IDD when she began her roommate matching service. She spent ten years working for King County Housing and Community Development Division in Seattle, and seven years as housing coordinator for King County Developmental Disabilities Division, where she experienced firsthand the struggles families faced:

> One of the significant emotional events that guided my career was when I was working in housing. I heard a story of a man with disabilities who was sixty-five years old. He had lived in the same house with his mom his whole life. He knew his neighbors and they all looked out for him. One evening a neighbor found him wandering the neighborhood. She picked him up and took him home to find his mom dead on the floor. This gentleman was taken to

a state institution because there was nobody to care for him. He lost his mom and the only life he'd ever known in one day.

When Pam Blanton repeated this story to me, she said, "My hair still stands up on the back of my neck when I think about that." Hearing about this tragedy made her want to make a difference for families because unfortunately, the scenario of unprepared families without a housing option in place is all too common:

> All the parents I talk to are worried about what is going to happen when they die. Seventy percent of adults with IDD live with family. Twenty-four percent of their caregivers are over age 60. The need is huge and growing fast. Families cannot wait for a government solution. They must be proactive and figure it out on their own.

Pam believes this is her calling: "Many families are out there trying to find a solution, and I want to help them."

The moment she began working as housing coordinator in Seattle, people were asking Pam about roommate matching. People would say, "If we could find compatible roommates, we could make this happen. We could share the cost of housing and services." She approached government agencies and local not-for-profits to encourage them to start a room-mate matching program, but no one was interested. Understanding the magnitude of the need, she decided to leave her job, start Partners4Housing and develop a roommate matching program.

Because she had already identified the problem, in the next phase of her company's development, she started to research what would make people compatible to live together. She tackled the question by looking specifically at college roommate matching services and dating sites, and her research culminated in Partners4Housing's Residential Assessment. The assessment was designed to identify a person's favorite activities, their gifts and strengths, their lifestyle preferences, their support needs, what services they had in place, and their overall housing vision.

The 127 questions are based on years of experience and include:

- Does your family member have social security?
- Does your family member have Medicaid-funded Person Care services from the state?
- What are your family member's favorite activities in the home?
- What are their favorite community activities?
- What is your vision of a good life for your family member?

- What spiritual background is your family member accustomed to?
- What is their vision of a good day?
- What do they do on a typical day?

The assessment also includes questions to determine family compatibility as well as roommate compatibility. Pam recognized that while it's important for roommates to be compatible, it is equally important for families to be compatible because families who share a vision and values are essential for success.

Once families began submitting the Residential Assessments, Pam realized that many families did not have all the services to which they were entitled. "Service systems are so complicated, and it's very difficult for families to navigate." The Residential Assessment evolved into a first-step planning tool, and because of her years of working in government, Pam was able to help families navigate across multiple social service systems to maximize their family member's benefits. Only after families have completed the Residential Assessment are they invited to join the roommate matching pool. This assessment ensures that they are ready for this next step in the housing process.

As she increased her clientele and pool of individuals seeking roommates in Washington, she was still carrying out the matching exercise by hand as she tried to find investors to fund a pseudo "match.com," the online platform she envisioned which members could use to find each other. However, when it came to developing the platform, she thought to herself, "I don't know what I need, I'm a social worker." Therefore, when her business coach determined a tentative cost for developing the service, she accepted that number as the amount she needed to raise.As she began to speak with investors, the cost seemed more and more insurmountable: "I couldn't find any investors because investors didn't really understand the need. Unless you have a family member with a disability or you know somebody, most people just don't understand the magnitude of the need."

She completed a start-up bootcamp run by one organization which ended with a pitch to investors in order to get capital. When she finally gave her pitch, "I got an award for my pitch, everybody thought it was a great idea, but they didn't give me any money."

Other investors continued to turn her down as she tried to raise capital, but while talking to a friend about the problem, they suggested "maybe you just need a different website." Exploring this path, Pam decided to recruit a developer herself and put a description of the project's scope on LinkedIn, "I decided to get bids and see what other people think this will cost. In the end, I met a web developer who understood the need and wanted to be part of the solution." At the end of 2018, after five years of doing roommate matching by hand, the web developer realized her vision, and Partners4Housing launched an online platform for roommate matching.

However, the platform acts as just one resource provided by Partners4Housing to establish the ideal Shared Living home:

> Roommate matching is a tool. The goal is a Shared Living home. Shared Living is a family-driven housing model. It's created for people by those who know them best… . their family. Each home is unique to the individuals living in the home.

In addition to providing roommate matching, Partners4Housing also guides families through the process of setting up a Shared Living home. Since 2014, she has helped families create 30 homes serving 65 individuals:

> The essence of our model is that compatible families commit to working together to identify and secure appropriate housing and services, and they collaborate to make the shared solution successful.

The roommate matching platform is now available in Washington and Arizona for use, but still, "I get calls and emails and hits through my website every day," Pam said.

People are constantly contacting her asking, "When are you coming to New Jersey?" "We're in Texas and we need a roommate," or "We're in California." As of 2019, she is continuing to offer roommate matching and shared living development services with the goal of making her services available nationwide.

**

It can seem that all the pathways leading to independent housing are blocked. However, these organizations demonstrate that forging your own path can be practical and attainable, and you need not travel alone.

CHAPTER 4:

CHOICE

—

Although group homes may be the most common housing option and the focus of this book, they are not the right option for everyone. As housing for people with IDD becomes more community based, oftentimes the fear of repeating the past creates problems for the future.

The Centers for Medicare & Medicaid Services (CMS) provides funding for long term services for individuals with IDD through Home & Community-Based Service (HCBS) waivers. In 2009, they began to develop regulations to determine which organizations could receive these waivers, and they outlined the requirements in the HCBS final settings rule in 2014.[40] In the rule, CMS stated that they are "moving

---

40 "Learn about the Issues." *Coalition for Community Choice.*

away from defining home and community-based settings by "what they are not," and toward defining them by the nature and quality of individuals' experiences."[41]

While this suggested they would provide funding to a wide variety of settings if they were right for the residents, in the months after the final setting rule, CMS released a document that defined settings which they considered isolating for residents with IDD. In the document, they identify farmsteads, gated/secured communities, residential schools, and multiple settings co-located and operationally related as settings which "are presumed to have institutional qualities and do not meet the rule's requirements for home and community-based settings."[42]

It is easy to be wary of communities with a population made primarily up of people with IDD because history has shown the dangers of segregation (see Chapter 1: Evolution from Institutionalization to Group Housing). However, these regulations show that when policy-makers live in fear of repeating the past, they create unintentional negative consequences for the future. Every community will be different,

---

41 "Fact Sheet: Summary of Key Provisions of the Home and Community-Based Services (HCBS) Settings Final Rule." *Centers for Medicare and Medicaid Services,* January 10, 2014.

42 "Guidance on Settings That Have the Effect of Isolating Individuals Receiving HCBS from the Broader Community." *Centers for Medicare and Medicaid Services.*

and many of the settings listed above are positive options for some individuals.

In order to ensure the United States does not fall back into trying to provide a one-size-fits-all model, many advocates have spoken out on the importance of providing a variety of housing options. For example, Coalition for Community Choice has begun the process of educating people on the benefits of different models. Along with Together for Choice, they have fought against legislative and regulatory change that limits choice. Also, Point Rider, Inc. has helped families develop housing options of their choice.As stated best by self-advocate and member of the Coalition for Community Choice, Susan Jennings, "Denying choice of living arrangements to individuals with disabilities is a denial of their civil rights."[43]

COALITION FOR COMMUNITY CHOICE

In her time working at the Madison House Autism Foundation, the organization funded Desiree Kameka's travels throughout the country to visit group homes, intentional communities, adult foster systems, institutional settings and everything in between to see the housing options out there and expand her Autism Housing Network database. As she

---

43   "Our Voices." *Coalition for Community Choice.*

continued to look, she noticed that often barriers to funding or developing different models stemmed not from the organizations and communities themselves but from larger governing bodies:

> That's when I realized that there was certainly some gaps in policy where people were having trouble doing what they felt was the best solution in their local community because policy was creating unintended consequences.

In response, Desiree began to look for other ways to enable people to create housing options that are not just centered around community expectations but instead what is right for the individual. Along with 15 other advocates, Desiree founded the Coalition for Community Choice (CCC) in January 2014, and she now serves as the national coordinator for the organization. The official goal of the CCC is to connect advocates across the country and help people make changes to policy based on what is best for them, not the state.

When I asked Desiree about how CCC takes action, she asked me to name my state. When I told her I was in Maryland, she immediately replied, "just up the road from you, in New Jersey, there was a policy recommendation proposal that would have limited options." The state government was telling advocates, "Medicaid is not going to fund farmsteads or anything

over six people living together, or disability communities."
Advocates from New Jersey contacted Desiree, and asked,
"Will you help us educate people so that they can become
advocates?"From there, Desiree traveled to New Jersey to
introduce the wider community to the potential for larger
housing options: "I did presentations and I showed them
examples of farmsteads around the country that exist and
are fantastic and are the types of settings that New Jersey
said was not possible."She told the people who were oppos-
ing the legislation to ask the question, "Why is New Jersey
restricting it if it's possible in other states, and it's not breaking federal law?'" Because of the advocacy practiced by the
individuals, they blocked the legislation, so that they could
keep providing care for individuals in larger settings. "It is
a really big, great win, right for their community."

When Desiree finished explaining this example to me, she
went on to share a specific project that the CCC helped
launch. Several families in Miami had joined together to
create a housing solution called Casa Familia. Casa Familia
is a plan for an intentional community in which people
with and without IDD can live and whose goal is to provide
affordable quality housing for people with developmental disabilities.

To help the newly founded group advocate for their idea
within their wider community, Desiree went to Miami, and

she did a presentation in their local theater about the positive effects of intentional communities nationwide:Because of their advocacy, and doing the presentation about best practices across the country and how they were proposing to incorporate so many of these best practices, we were able to get a planning branch to launch their project, which is really exciting.

In both of her stories, Desiree shows how ultimately being educated and educating others on the issues at hand and the different housing options available can help the variety of these communities continue to develop and thrive. Like the Autism Housing Network, the goal of the CCC is to start that conversation and to educate.

They also provide information targeted to how people whose living situation is at risk can advocate about why they should not lose funding. Specifically, they help individuals and organizations make sure that the programs do not violate the Olmstead decision, which prohibits unjustified segregation of individuals with IDD.

Desiree is widely regarded as the leading expert on disability housing, and of course, that means a lot of people want to know the right answer in housing:

I get a lot of contacts from the Autism Housing Network, oftentimes parents, and they want to know what's the best model out there, and I cannot tell them because I don't know who that future resident is. I don't know what their preferences are. I don't know what their support needs are. I don't know what type of funding they collect. And so it's really important when we are looking at solutions, we stay person centered.

TOGETHER FOR CHOICE

Mark Olson, a co-founder of the Coalition for Community Choice, began thinking about adult housing options when he became a single parent in 2007 to his daughter Lindsay, who has autism. "My friends came to me and they said, 'What happens to Lindsay when you're not around?'"

Luckily, Mark may have had one of the best backgrounds to begin his search for housing options: "I used to be an investigative reporter, and I used to be a marketing consultant, so I know how to get smart on topics really fast. I just started digging in." He went into everything: "Well, what would happen if I wasn't around? Where would she go? What would that look like? How would it get paid for? So on and so forth." Although he found many group homes and farmsteads that looked fine, none seemed to fit the specific interests and needs of Lindsay.That is when he began developing a live/ work/play housing model known as LTO Ventures which was his vision for Lindsay's ideal housing option based on her abilities, disabilities, and the desires she expressed for the life she wanted to live. To help create the model, he continued to visit homes and read up on housing options: "I probably read 100,000 words a day online, so I'm reading research papers, I'm reading business plans, etc." When he went to visit homes, he did so as a parent, an entrepreneur, and an emerging expert. "I'd go visit a new place, and I'd take a tour, and I would just ask them tons and tons of questions as we did the walk through."

As he began receiving answers, he found that often one organization's problem could be solved by another group he visited. For example, sometimes a representative at one housing option would say, "We've got all these things figured out, but we can't figure out this one problem. This is the thing that's really kind of making us crazy." After a while, he would be able to respond, "Wait a minute, I just was at another place that solves that problem. Let me connect the two of you together, and you can talk about solutions."

As Mark continued to make connections between different housing options, he became recognized as an expert in the field, and similar to Desiree, "I just started putting together presentations on housing and employment." What was so

fascinating about giving the presentations was that he continued to see a disconnect between organizations. He would go
to one organization that had one housing option, and upon
hearing about different options, the parents and staff in the
room would say, "We have no idea what you're talking about.
Never heard of any of this." Then when he visited parents and
staff at other settings, they would say, "We have no idea about
any of the other settings you're talking about."

In 2014, he was one of the fifteen advocates who helped
found the Coalition for Community Choice, and then
Together for Choice (TFC), a coalition which emerged from
CCC. Together for Choice focuses on finding and ending
policy which limits the choice of housing and employment
options. Like Desiree, he believes that education and ending
the disconnect between different organizations is the key to
ensure choice:

> I think the more and more we talk about it helps
> create awareness. It points people to other resources.
> It validates a lot of these concepts. I think it's criti-
> cally important.

POINT RIDER INC.

In addition to his work with CCC and Together for Choice,
in 2019, Mark created a nonprofit, Point Rider, Inc. with

Jerry Horton, founder of Down Home Ranch, a farmstead in Texas,. The company goes around the country to help families and nonprofits develop housing solutions. While families may have an idea of what housing option they want, they frequently do not know where to begin:

> They're all starting with a blank sheet of paper, and so what we say to them is, don't start with a blank sheet of paper, start with people who've done it before.

They begin their work with the families and organizations by asking about their vision. Then, he and his partner take the families through a workshop they call "kickstarting your dream." "It's a very intense one-day workshop, where we're essentially helping them to determine if they are viable and if their vision is viable, and then we lay out what it's going to take to do it." After giving them an in-depth assessment of what will happen in development, the families can then decide if they want to continue with the process. They can also decide whether they want Point Rider to drive the project or just act as consultants in different areas. No matter what they decide, because of the support the organization has provided, "the idea is to save them hundreds of thousands of dollars and several years to try and do it on their own."

In addition to helping families develop new housing solutions, Point Rider classifies and publishes information about existing and emerging housing settings around the country in a taxonomy of models. While ultimately, they imagine about ten different categories in the taxonomy, the main categories currently include independent shared homes, shared home neighborhoods, apartment complexes, farmsteads and ranches, and mixed-use campuses (live-work-play). Point Rider plans to turn their experience and knowledge of the categories and many individual settings into an array of eight to ten "playbooks" that document how to create each model type from conception to occupancy.

When discussing the key to increasing housing solutions, Mark explained:

> I have one particular view of how I want to make this happen. I have tons and tons of friends who are also developing communities, and they have different ideas on how they want to do it. So if you support choice, and you share innovative ideas with each other, people are going to come up and they're going to think about new options and new designs, new solutions. In that way, you're going to increase the variety of settings, and also the number of them.

Because of the work of CCC and TFC along with other advocates throughout the country, in March 2019, the CMS created new guidelines that revoked the claims that certain communities of people primarily living with IDD were isolating. Instead, they determined that the factors which indicate that a setting is isolating and should not receive HCBS waivers are:

- Due to the design or model of service provision in the setting, individuals have limited, if any, opportunities for interaction in and with the broader community, including with individuals not receiving Medicaid-funded HCBS;
- The setting restricts beneficiary choice to receive services or to engage in activities outside of the setting;
- The setting is physically located separate and apart from the broader community and does not facilitate beneficiary opportunity to access the broader community and participate in community services, consistent with a beneficiary's person-centered service plan.[44]

This guidance shifts the focus to the needs of each individual in determining whether the setting works for them.

While in an article relating the victory, TFC states they are optimistic about the increased accessibility to HCBS waivers

---

44 "Home and Community-Based Settings Regulation – Heightened Scrutiny" *Centers for Medicare and Medicaid Services,* March 22, 2019.

for which this guidance will allow, they are going to continue to push to make the guidance a part of the rule:

> A Rule has greater permanence; a future administration can revoke this new guidance and reinstate the old guidance. For these reasons, TFC will continue to push for legislative changes to the Medicaid statute to ensure that CMS honors individual choice and recognizes a broad array of options to meet the needs of individuals with disabilities.[45]

There is still a disconnect between the policymakers on housing for people with IDD and the people affected by their policy, but by making a voice for themselves, CCC and TFC continue to make choice a priority on paper and in practice.

---

45 Mendal, Scott. "CMS Issues New Guidance on its Settings Rule." *Together for Choice*, June 6, 2019.

DESIGN INTRODUCTION

The Center for Applied Disability Research defines the ideal design of group homes for people with IDD as homes with the following characteristics:[46]

- six or fewer residents
- sufficient staff size (based on number of residents)
- compatible roommates
- houses which blend in with other houses in the surrounding neighborhood

---

46 Bigby, C. and E Bould. "Guide to Good Group Homes, Evidence about what makes the most difference to the quality of group homes." *Centre for Applied Disability Research*, 2017.

I would like to consider these principles the base for a successful group home structure (although there are many other different types of successful housing options which may not have these characteristics). From there, group homes can optimize the structure by implementing different practices.

In the following chapters, I will highlight three different practices being used to improve the base characteristics of an ideal group home design. The practices include developments in smart home technology, universal design, and health information collection, respectively, and all of the practices can be expanded and implemented in different ways in group homes and other housing options nationwide.

Although some innovations require large amounts of capital and technology and will take years before they can be implemented nationally, all of these stories demonstrate how small changes can also greatly increase individuals' quality of life.

CHAPTER 5:

SMART HOME TECHNOLOGY

Different technological innovations have been revolution-ary for people both with cognitive and physical disabilities. Computer-based therapy exists for individuals with autism.[47] People in wheelchairs can get around with increased ease and efficiency in motorized chairs, and many people who cannot move their arms have head switches to control the chairs.[48] Even my own brother, Robb, benefits from tech-nology, and because of his speaking tablet, he can now con-tribute to the conversation by clicking on pictures which say different words.

---

47   Herskowitz, Valerie. "Computer-Based Therapy for Autistic Chil-dren" *Organization for Autism Research,* January 1, 2003.

48   "Power Wheelchair Drive Controls." *Mobilitybasics.Ca.*

While there is now so much technology to help individuals themselves, what can be done to improve the houses in which people live? This question was asked by Imagine!, a group home provider, whose goal is to increase the use of technology in the disability housing sector through the creation of smart homes.[49]

The label "smart home" seems to connote a futuristic or elitist idea. For me, the term immediately brings to mind movies about a billionaire's house or a dystopian society where AI rules the word. However, today, we all have technology in our homes to enhance quality of life, and smart homes represent just one technological advancement toward optimizing the efficiency and convenience of houses.

As defined by Coldwell Banker:

> The term smart home describes homes equipped with lighting, heating and other connected devices that can be controlled remotely by smartphone or computer, and often communicate with each other.[50]

---

49 "What's In Your Cabinet?" *Then Again, What Do I Know?* October 10, 2018.
50 "Smart Homes: An Emerging Real Estate Opportunity" *Coldwell Banker.* 2018.

IMAGINE! SMART HOME

In 2009, Imagine! launched the first smart home in the country designed for people with intellectual and developmental disabilities in Boulder, Colorado, with the goal of utilizing technology as effectively as possible to increase quality of life.

When walking through the smart home, a visitor may not notice major differences between this home and other group homes. Visitors will find the house inconspicuously located in a neighborhood with the most obvious benefit being a bus station in walking distance.

Upon entering the house, like many group homes, there are also elements of universal design, small changes which also allow for improved livelihood for the residents. For example, the open floor plan allows individuals in wheelchairs, like Donna and Gerald Fairchild, two residents of the smart home, to move throughout the house easily, and the light switches are all situated low on the wall so Donna and Gerald can turn lights on and off independently. (For more information on universal design, see Chapter 9: Design Empathy)

What may seem out of the ordinary is that on one side of the door, visitors will find a card holder. Residents and caregivers carry cards with them at all times around the house. These cards use radio-frequency identification to indicate when caregivers and residents have entered or left the house, and they also give information about where the caregiver or the resident is in the house. Caregivers and residents can access this information by logging into one of the many computers situated throughout the house. Because all residents have the card, the caregiver is alerted whenever an individual leaves the house or if a resident has fallen and may require medical attention. Also, residents can use the card to contact the caregivers whenever they are in need of assistance.

However, the card not only provides communication and one-time alerts, but it can also collect data on the residents to assist the caregivers. One of the employees at the smart home in Colorado described it by saying: "Technology is so ingrained in the design that people kind of communicate with the house. The house can give you feedback."

For example, if a very social resident is spending more time than usual in his room, then the caregivers will be alerted about the behavior, and they can check in with the resident to determine if the change has more serious roots.

*Note: Since I researched Imagine! in spring 2019, they have begun to phase out the radio frequency identification cards and have been instead using smart phones which can take over many of the tasks at a fraction of the cost. After discovering the capabilities of the card system at the front door, visitors will discover uses of technology as they continue through the house. In the kitchen, an adjustable table and sink allows residents in wheelchairs to wash dishes, eat, or prepare meals without staff supervision. The visitors might also find residents watching the television screen in the kitchen as it gives step-by-step instructions to help more independent residents cook their own meals.

On recounting visitors' reactions to the smart home, Donna laughingly commented:

> It's kind of funny when people visit the smart home, and with all the different technology that's here, the one thing they all sure are impressed with is the size of our TV. I guess it's something that everyone can relate to.

After walking through the kitchen, the visitor can then go on to look at one of the eight bedrooms in the house where even individuals lacking the fine motor skills to operate light switches can turn the lights on and off and open and close blinds through their personal tablets.

When asked to describe her experience in the smart home, Donna explains: "Instead of living in a place where people have to take care of me, I now have a place to call home where I can do more things for myself."

Along with the obvious benefits of self-empowerment and efficiency, the ability for increased independence also transforms the relationship with the staff. Staff members can focus on developing friendships with the residents rather than doing normal tasks like preparing meals or helping the residents move throughout the house.

In 2010, when the concept for the smart home was beginning to develop, Danette Muselman and Elizabeth Woodruff, students at the University of Colorado Denver decided to test the benefits of the smart home themselves and published *Changes in Quality of Life for Group Home Residents of the Bob and Judy Charles Smart Home: An Exploratory Analysis.* The study was designed to examine if the technology in the homes increased overall quality-of-life of the eight residents living there.

After doing five rounds of interview calls with residents before they entered the home and then after they had lived there for a year, they worked to examine the changes to quality of life using both questions from the National Core Indicator (NCI) Quality of Life scale and also questions about how the residents were utilizing the technology. The goal was to compare objective increases in quality of life with more subjective, specialized data. After comparing the data from the first and second interviews, they saw a clear indication of increased quality of life across the board.[51]

However, the benefits provided by the smart home come at a cost. While the use of solar panels and geothermal heating do lower the price of operation, the home still costs about $65,000 to provide services to each resident every year. Although the number is below the average cost per residents for private group homes which range from $90,000 to $140,000, the cost even after receiving state funding is not attainable for the vast majority of families.[52]

Therefore, the goal of the Imagine! Smart Home is not to create more houses, but instead, as stated by Imagine! executive Fred Hobbs, "What we're trying to do is identify and test in real world situations what kinds of technologies can help individuals with developmental disabilities engage in the community." They hope to expand the technology into different group homes or other living situations instead of expanding the smart house model.

51   Muselman, Dannette and Elizabeth Woodruff. *Changes in Quality of Life for Group Home Residents of the Bob and Judy Charles SmartHome: An Exploratory Analysis.* University of Colorado Denver, November 2010.

52   Kovner, Josh. "Bill Would Encourage Housing Options For Group Home Clients." *Hartford Courant,* March 23, 2018.

While working with technology, the company also remains flexible to constant adaptations. As Fred stated to me: "As technology continues to change, we continue to adapt... . smart homes are living, breathing entities."

LIVING RESOURCES SMART HOME

In 2014, Living Resources launched the first smart home in New York state modeled after the Imagine! Smart Home with the similar goal of experimenting with technology. They have become a hub for technological innovation both by finding new technology and repurposing other designs.

In the smart home, they use an Amazon Alexa to operate lights, shades, fans, and the television. In addition, they have added a Magnetic Induction cooktop to their kitchens which cooks food without flame and automatically turns off after a certain amount of time.[53]

They also work with a local university in order to research the different problems within the homes, and how they can use technology to solve them.

For caregivers, 61 percent of work injuries are due to accidents while lifting or moving residents, which raises the question:

---

53 "Smart Homes." *Living Resources.*

Can different positions increase risk? Caregivers conducted thirty-two transfers bed-to-bed and chair-to-chair with residents who were both partially and fully dependent. They used sensors throughout the body to track the movement of each individual, and then, they compared their movements to the lifting technique of a physical therapist.

The differences between caregivers and the physical therapist showed how common improper lifting techniques occurred, and they are currently using the data to develop sensors which alert workers that they are using an improper position. In 2019, Living Resources worked alongside The University at Albany and Human Condition Safety, a private company that creates wearable items to increase employee safety, in order to create items designed for caregivers. They plan to market the design to group homes throughout the country with the hope that they can decrease costs of work-injuries.[54]

**

As these smart homes continue to test new uses of technology, they hope individual organizations can adopt their techniques and even just look for creative ways to use technology created for the general public in group homes. One

---

54 "Designing a Wearable System for Prevention of Health Care Worker Injuries." *Xsens.*

of these technologies, which offers a plethora of opportunity, is Amazon Alexa.

In April 2019, Amazon Alexa unveiled the Alexa Skills Kit which allows individuals and organizations to create skills with Alexa either by coding it themselves, following a template provided by the company, or hiring an agency to realize their vision.[55] This program can allow families and group home providers to create custom commands for Alexa depending on a resident's needs.

Alongside their skills kit, Amazon Alexa also announced they are now HIPAA compliant which means that they can access and store patient information for health care providers nationwide. With this information available through the device, health care providers can make Alexa skills specific to health-care related needs. They already have six skills which have been developed alongside health companies including "Alexa, pull up my blood glucose readings," which was created for people with diabetes.[56]

This new feature of Alexa alone offers so many opportunities to develop targeted voice skills for group homes, and it shows that although an entire smart home can be

---

55   "Why Build Alexa Skills?" *Amazon Alexa.*
56   Farr, Christina. "'Alexa, find me a doctor': Amazon Alexa adds new medical skills." *CNBC,* April 4, 2019.

overwhelmingly expensive, new technologies being developed have the potential to help all people make their homes a little smarter.

CHAPTER 6:

DESIGN EMPATHY

———

Although smart homes may offer advanced technologies that can greatly improve the quality of life of residents, by looking at different basic features of home design, people can implement small changes which could make a world of difference in the overall quality of a home.

UNIVERSAL DESIGN

As defined by the National Center on Accessibility, universal design is,

The design of products and environments to be usable by all people, to the greatest extent possible, without the need for adaptation or specialized design.[57]

Universal design has become a concept used throughout the country to help create homes that fit the needs of the widest range of abilities, and it is a hallmark of group housing.

I first heard about the concept because it was used in a local home run by Bello Machre in Maryland. Although the front of the Bello Machre Sage Home looks like the rest in the neighborhood, there are indoor adjustments designed to better accommodate the four roommates with intellectual disabilities living there.

The house has 46-inch doors to accommodate Jamie and Joe who both use wheelchairs, and the countertops are only 34 inches off of the ground so that they can also exercise independence in the kitchen. There is an open floor plan and no carpeting to allow for ease of mobility for Jamie and Joe, and outside the house, the ramps on each of the porches seamlessly fit into the house's design.[58] These are

57 Connell, Bettye Rose, Mike Jones, Ron Mace, Jim Mueller, Abir Mullick, Elaine Ostroff, Jon Sanford, Ed Steinfeld, Molly Story, and Gregg Vanderheiden. "Principles of Universal Design." *National Center on Accessibility,* April 1, 1997.

58 Winters, Wendi. "Home of the Week: Home sweet home for four developmentally disabled residents and their caretakers." Capital Gazette, March 28, 2015.

just a few examples of the endless features which fall under universal design.

For additional examples of universal design in action along with the latest news in the field, visit universaldesign.com.

One new development in universal design, dubbed "design empathy," focuses on designing spaces for individuals with sensory sensitivity which is a common trait of people with autism and other neurological disorders.

SENSORY-SENSITIVITY DESIGN

AJ Paron-Wildes started her career as an interior designer, but her inspiration to research design in connection with autism took root in 1998 when her son, Devin was diagnosed with the disorder.

Devin had developed normally as a baby, but as a toddler, he began to lose social skills he had only just started to develop. By the time he turned 3, AJ struggled because,

> "He couldn't talk... . he had no eye contact... . I couldn't touch him, I could not hug him, I could not be connected with him in any way shape or form."

When describing her son's diagnosis and inability to connect, AJ admitted, "I was angry. I was upset. I had lost this child. I was mad at myself. I wasn't a doctor. I wasn't a speech therapist. I wasn't all these people that he needed." However, AJ was determined to make her son's life as positive as possible, and she decided to educate herself on everything about the spectrum. Specifically, she began to read books about the autism experience including a book by Temple Grandin, a self-advocate who shares her life story. The book, Thinking in Pictures, would change the course of AJ's career.

In the book, Temple talks about her connection with the environment, and the increased sensitivity she and many other people with autism have to the world around them. While reading it, AJ states:

> What struck me was how their senses experienced the world. Everything was so different in how they saw things as far as colors, lighting, vibrancy. The whole notion of how they experience the environment was totally different. That intrigued me.

A.J. had been a designer throughout her career, but she had never before considered how the designs would affect other viewers because "As a designer, you design to the normalcy of your senses." However, with this book, she realized that if people have different sensory experiences, their reactions to her designs will be vastly different from her own.

Upon contacting Cynthia Leibrock, a leader in the field of universal design, AJ discovered that no one had conducted research specifically on universal design targeted toward people with autism. And so, with the help of graduate students and professors from the University of Minnesota, AJ began a research program with the end goal of creating design principles for individuals on the spectrum.AJ is now recognized as the leading expert in Design Empathy, and she has written three books compiling her research. In addition, she has developed designs for children in school, adults in the workplace, adult group-homes, and more. Throughout her work, she continues to show that: "Design is meaningful and design can impact an outcome."

For example, AJ describes one experience early in her career when she volunteered to design the environment for adults with autism in a controlled workspace. When showing one of the women working in the facility different potential wall paint colors, every time the employee saw the color swatch she would begin repeating the name of another color. For example, when AJ showed her a light green sage they wanted to use, the woman immediately began repeating red.

When considering how sensory sensitivity could have a role in her reactions, AJ realized that "every color I showed her she saw the afterimage color."[59] Afterimage color is the complementary color to the one someone is looking at, and afterimages can be caused by looking at one color for a very long time. For many people with sensory sensitivity, the afterimage is amplified.[60]

To help ensure that the wall paint did not produce a strong afterimage for the woman, the designers experimented with a variety of different colors. Eventually, "we found a neutral gray and showed it to her and she didn't say anything. We were like that's the one we're doing." In many situations, the design choices for people with sensory sensitivities may seem extremely dull: neutral colors and minimal furniture. However, these patterns ensure people with sensory sensitivities are not overwhelmed by the design. AJ's designs have a positive reception from the sensory-sensitive individuals who she serves.

Although AJ's work focuses on autism, the concept of design empathy and universal design continues to gain momentum. As people work to integrate group homes into the community,

59 "AJ Paron-Wildes :: Design Empathy – Hatch Festival 2013." *Hatch Experience,* February 22, 2014.
60 Cherry, Kendra. "Positive and Negative Afterimages." *VeryWell Mind,* June 22, 2019.

this design has helped to make residents' experiences as positive as possible.

Ultimately, AJ explains:

> "Especially as designers, just because we design a system, a space, an element, a place, just because this is how we interpret it, that's not necessarily how someone else interprets it. They might see the color differently, it might be too intense for them."[61]

**

While my brother Robb is at the other end of the sensory sensitivity spectrum and has reduced sensitivity, I think this information is crucial to any families looking for a group home regardless of whether their loved one has physical disabilities and/or sensory sensitivity. It addresses the fact that everyone sees the world differently and has different preferences.

There were a few years during which Robb refused to wear striped shirts. While no one else in my family had anything against stripes, we respected his opinion, and he stuck to solid colors. When deciding on a color for Robb's room, Robb

---

61 "AJ Paron-Wildes :: Design Empathy – Hatch Festival 2013." *Hatch Experience,* February 22, 2014.

may have an opinion about which color is best. He also might not care. We will only know his preferences by ensuring he is as active as he can be at every level of the decision-making process (although I am pretty sure we will be steering clear of any striped designs).

CHAPTER 7:

PROCEDURAL DESIGN

—

In 2017, one company decided to design a "smart home," but instead of changing the houses themselves, they changed the very set-up of data collection in the group homes. Even when the changes were intangible in nature, residents could see the results.

MID-ATLANTIC GIGABIT INNOVATION COLLABORATORY

If most of us have not heard the term "medical decision loop" before, almost all of us know about the process which happens when we go to the doctor's office. Upon entering the examination room, the doctor assesses our symptoms either through questions or physical inspection. (For me, I am just sitting there hoping they don't want to do a strep test.) They go on to analyze the data they have collected and then make some sort of decision about a potential treatment. Finally, they examine the results of the treatment and decide whether the treatment is working or a new plan is necessary. Whether this process is happening over minutes in an intensive care unit or over a matter of weeks or years during check-ups with your physician, the overall process is the same.

What if this process could take place constantly over a lifetime? Instead of specifically assessing problems after they have developed, professionals could target the problems as soon as or even before they arise. Then, they could use that data to help prevent future issues. What if all of this could happen in the home? The amount of trips to the doctor could decrease with increased health and overall well being for the residents.

In a partnership with Target Community & Educational Services, Inc., the Mid-Atlantic Gigabit Innovation Collaboratory (MAGIC), a nonprofit which supports technological innovation in Maryland, has decided to expand this medical decision loop into group homes.

Although constantly amassing data and then analyzing it may seem like a daunting task requiring large amounts of technology, a lot of what needs to be collected is not hard to do, it just has not been done before. In a presentation on the procedure, Dr. Robert Wack, President of MAGIC, described the data collection procedure, and the three groups of data they plan to collect:

1. "One is behavioral data that is entered by the staff in the homes that captures in a computable form the activities of daily living, the client's behavior, their moods, changes in their activity." For example, if a client has been sleeping for longer amounts of time than usual, the staff can take account of the activity. Because the homes in which the process is being implemented have staff checking-in daily or 24/7 care, they are constantly available to pick up on changes in a residents' behavior even if they do not themselves know what is causing the change.

2. "The second category is physiologic data. This is stuff that could be collected by a fit-bit or some sort of personal device: heart rate, respiratory rate, temperature, weight changes, activity level, how many steps, where they move around in the house." Like the first group of data, this type of data is easy to compiled but has just never been collected.

3. "The third category is environmental data: room temperature, noise, light level, etc."

None of these data pieces require advanced technology simply direct service providers (DSPs) collecting them.

The difficulty comes when localizing the data in a database. To address this next part of the medical decision loop, MAGIC will take the three sources of data and normalize it. From there, they will be able to move on to step three and put the information into a database. MAGIC has partnered with a data collection company called Skayl which will keep all of the data stored in an online cloud.

By having everything localized, all DSPs need to do is take a couple of minutes each day in order to start tracking the data, so that MAGIC has enough information to complete the final step: analysis. As described by Robert, "The fourth step is applying analytics to this database. That is addressing specific clinical problems in the home."

It's true that implementing this process with such a large amount of information could result in an overwhelming amount of solutions to problems which were not even relevant in the house. However, MAGIC is specializing and organizing the analysis to ensure quality information:

> This is where we are trying to take a very modular, a-la-carte, approach to the analytics. We don't want to try to throw a giant analytics engine at a home where really there are only two or three specific problems we need to look at. We are really trying to take, along with an open data approach to it, an

open analytics approach to it, so the analytics can be customized to specific problems in the home.

Maybe the room temperature is causing discomfort among the residents which affects their mood. Then the next question can be: How should the temperature be changed to better suit the residents?

Maybe a shift in the schedule has created increased engagement among members of the house. Then the staff can brainstorm: How can other changes continue to cultivate and strengthen relationships within the house or how can the relationships be maintained?

As the loop continues, the staff will have data from years past, so that they can see if any of the things that worked well then could be used in the present. Also, new staff can have a better sense of the residents with whom they are going to work by examining the in-depth medical history.

Although this process started with just two homes two years ago, the residents have already had decreased emergency room, urgent care, and doctor visits along with an overall decrease in staff time spent addressing medical issues. The company hopes that these benefits are just the start.

Robert explains that the goal is "eventually building a community of these homes which allows us to tackle community health problems which right now we don't have the resources or the data for. We may be able to create analytics to create new things." With this project, MAGIC has the potential not only to collect data in order to improve individual group homes, but also to improve the conditions of group homes at a national level by finding the large scale problems.

This process is still in its beginning stages, and implementing the MAGIC system into different homes does require capital to fund databases and analysis companies, which for most group home providers and families is not feasible. However, while the high-tech process developed by MAGIC cannot be utilized in all homes, group homes can use the medical-loop procedure to target problems within their group homes.

Ultimately, the process requires caregivers to take note of data, so that if problems are identified in the home, they can use that information to find a solution. It may only take ten or fifteen minutes a day, but the long term results include savings in time and money and overall healthier residents.[62]

---

62 "MAGIC's Smart Home Presentation 8/28/2017." *MAGIC,* August 31, 2017.

STAFF/ RESIDENT RELATIONSHIPS INTRODUCTION

What makes or breaks a group home or any housing situation?

To answer this question, I spoke to representatives from organizations throughout the country, and I have received the same answer every time. As stated by Kristine Heuer, Assistant Director of Community Living from The Arc Carroll County, a branch of The Arc US, "It's the staff, it's 100 percent the staff. If the staff can find ways to connect with the people that they are working with and are open minded to letting people try new things and go places, that makes a world of difference."[63] The staff are the people that are going to be spending their days and often nights with residents in group homes and for many residents, staff members will be helping them in every aspect of their life.The following chapters will touch on how different approaches to cultivating a particular staff attitude, a community culture, and hiring practices, respectively, can help to enrich staff/resident relationships.

All of the stories demonstrate that ultimately, as stated by the Center for Applied Disability Research, "All communication in the house by staff should be warm and respectful." This means that caregivers are trying to help the residents be the best versions of themselves. They are actively supporting members of the group home to develop skills rather than completing tasks for the residents, and they individualize how they help different residents because every relationship will look different.

This respect must be present at every level, from caregivers or direct support professionals (DSPs) to the company CEO. Every person involved needs to be active in promoting good practices and holding people accountable for bad ones.

---

63 Bigby, C. and E. Bould. "Guide to Good Group Homes, Evidence about what makes the most difference to the quality of group homes." *Centre for Applied Disability Research*, 2017.

As Kristine states, oftentimes determining the quality of different staff is not a complex process, instead, "It's just seeing people at events, seeing the interactions, or even just through a conversation with the staff person and seeing the way that they're responding to you." The difficulty comes in implementing practices in a way that ensures that when you do see them at events, in interactions, in conversation, you are finding that the staff are actively helping to elevate the quality of life of the individuals in the homes.

CHAPTER 8:

STAFF ATTITUDE

While how staff care for and treat an individual with IDD is a key factor in the quality of group living, one question of the utmost importance is often overlooked: How do group home staff members view the residents The group home crisis in Jacksonville, Illinois, juxtaposed with a group home provider in Santa Clara County, California show how the attitude and mentality of the staff are a deciding factor in determining the quality of living in a particular group home.

ILLINOIS GROUP HOME TRAGEDY

When, in April 2012, Illinois governor Pat Quinn, began the process of deinstitutionalization with the Jacksonville Developmental Center, Illinois Department of Human Service officials presented a future of increased independence, community integration, and a home-like environment while still including the 24/7 care provided in institutions. However, from the start, deinstitutionalization was in reality a process of dehumanization for the individuals with IDD living in Illinois.

Art Dykstra, the former director of a group home provider in the area, recalls going to the Jacksonville Developmental Center for the "auction." A state official would describe peoples' disabilities and medical histories, and representatives from different group homes raised their hands whenever they heard about an individual for whom they wanted to provide housing. People who were higher functioning were the first to get providers. The "auction" immediately transformed people into mere objects and simplified their existence into one attribute making it easy for the people present to trivialize the residents' futures.[64]

Illinois is consistently listed as one of the five states providing the least amount of funding to people with IDD, and the influx of individuals into the system only increased the problem.[65] Caregivers were difficult to find and seemingly

---

64 Berens, Michael J. and Patricia Callahan. "In the rush to close institutions, Illinois glossed over serious problems in group homes." *Chicago Tribune,* December 30, 2016.

65 Berens, Michael J. and Patricia Callahan. "In Illinois group homes, adults with disabilities suffer in secret." *Chicago Tribune,* December 30, 2016.

impossible to retain which meant homes hired them quickly and often required no experience. While the Center for Applied Disability Research named "practice of staff" as one of the factors which makes the most difference in increasing the quality of a group home, many of these group homes in Illinois proved that the reverse was true also.[66]

When Thomas Powers and his family were told he was going to move to a group home, the change sparked hope for greater individualized care alongside more independence for Thomas, who would live outside of an institution for the first time since he was 6. However, in the first group home he entered, the untrained caregivers claimed he was "out of control" and too difficult for them to handle, and the organization moved him to another home with a fewer number of residents.

The family was not told that he was moving to a house declared "not approved for occupancy" by state officials. Three days after moving into the house, Thomas was found lying dead in a room on a soiled mattress filled with debris and various storage boxes. Although the state determined that he had experienced neglect from his caregiver, no steps

---

66 Bigby, C. and E. Bould. "Guide to Good Group Homes, Evidence about what makes the most difference to the quality of group homes." *Centre for Applied Disability Research*, 2017.

were taken to hold the wrongdoer accountable or even require additional supervision of the group home provider.

Thomas' death was not the only instance of neglect by an Illinois provider and its caregivers, and it marked just one of the over 2,000 cases of documented harm in group homes that occurred from 2010 to 2016. Other instances include untrained employees in one home taking part in "breaking" the residents, an activity in which they taunted the residents for their own personal amusement. In another house not far away, a caregiver fatally beat a resident under the pretense that they had stolen food, and like Powers' death, the employee received no punishment.

These problems were only revealed to the public by an investigative journalist's report "Suffering in Silence" published by the Chicago Tribune in 2016.

Parents, advocates, group home service providers, and the state have begun the process of improving group homes and creating more stringent regulation of group homes in Illinois. However, the problems in Illinois epitomize how two groups of people determine the success of group homes: direct support providers and the higher-up group home staff regulating them. These people play a crucial role in developing or destroying the quality of life of residents in group homes.[67]

**

After I first read about the horrific events in Illinois, I began to think about all of the people who work with my brother who I do not really know. I've never met some of the faculty and staff at his school who have contact with him, as well as many volunteers at the different activities and camps he attends outside of school. It took months to build a relationship even with the people who work most closely with my brother, like his school one-on-one and state-funded DSPs, to whom I feel very close now.

What if someone who works with my brother is not treating him with respect and dignity or actively causes him pain? Apart from someone noticing visible signs of distress in my brother's expression or manner when he is around that person or actual physical marks, there is really no way for us to know.

This fact became extremely apparent to my family when the principal at a previous school called to say a teacher had

---

67 Berens, Michael J. and Patricia Callahan. "In Illinois group homes, adults with disabilities suffer in secret." *Chicago Tribune*, December 30, 2016.

been fired for making inappropriate comments to a colleague about my brother while helping him use the bathroom. We have no idea if these comments came from more serious roots or if there are any other occurrences where this kind of behavior was not reported.

Like all families of people with IDD, we have to put so much faith in the people with whom my brother works, and when Robb moves out of my parents' house, this faith will have to increase as the primary caregiving duties move completely into DSPs' hands. However, when we experienced the guilt and sadness which comes when hearing Robb may not even be safe with staff at his own school and hearing stories about the group homes in Illinois, the idea of him moving out of the house only generates more fear.

LIFE SERVICES ALTERNATIVES

Because of the protectiveness I feel for my brother, I was wary when I first heard about how Dana Hooper, the executive director of a group home provider in California, cultivates a positive DSP/resident relationship by diverting from the mindset of prevention to promotion. However, as Dana explained to me, the only way to maximize the quality of life of the residents is to focus on how to be better than the minimum required by regulation and to promote growth and independence rather than solely preventing negative practices.

When Dana first made the decision to become executive director of Life Services Alternatives (LSA) in 2007, California was in a state of major change. Similar to the situation in Jacksonville, Illinois, the local institutional facility was closing in Santa Clara County, and his organization was selected to add additional capacity in the community. The organization began a rapid expansion, growing from three homes in 2007 to twelve homes with over 180 staff members by 2019.

While Life Services Alternatives group homes may, on the outside, look like other group homes, what makes the place so original is its commitment to quality. As Dana explains, in the community of people with IDD, "Most everything is geared around, preventing bad things from happening as opposed to supporting and encouraging good things."

To increase the positivity within his own organization he has focused on the latter.

When Dana was looking for a home for his own son with IDD, at the beginning of the process, he said, "A really loving home was always what I wanted." However, as he went to tour homes, not only did none of them seem loving, but most of them were homes Dana himself could not even imagine living in.

While developing the LSA homes, Dana knew that meeting the minimum requirements should not be the goal, and instead, they needed to look beyond government regulation to determine how to make residents' lives as meaningful as possible. At the core of this undertaking was the staff.

Dana identifies one of the key factors of creating a supportive staff as having, "an emerging sense of family. Their full time job was to care for these individuals, and so they developed relationships and it wasn't just a job." Like any family, the staff will still be protective of the residents and ensure they are not subject to harm, but they will also want to see the residents succeed and grow.

When examining how to cultivate a familial environment, Dana continued to return to their process for hiring staff. He wanted to ensure that the staff was self-selecting. That meant when someone walked into an interview with Dana, he took an unorthodox approach:

> In the past when I worked for technology startup companies we would try really hard to attract good candidates by selling them on the company: 'It's not just a good product its a great product. It's not just a good environment, it's a really great environment.' Often this resulted in the job and company

not living up to their expectations. At LSA, we do the exact opposite.

Instead of trying to convince people about the quality of the group homes and the value of the job, he would tell the candidates about the immense responsibility they would take on with the job. In doing this, "We start out with making sure that the candidate really understands what's entailed and what's going to be expected of them." In giving people a realistic expectation of their work, they are agreeing to take on the responsibility required to improve someone else's quality of life, and in the end, "They don't take it just because it is a job."

By having individuals who know what is expected, they can ensure that lasting relationships are being built which in turn leads to higher retention rates. (In 2018, the full-time employee turnover rate was under half the national average at 13 percent.) Ultimately, for Dana, from individuals living in the homes all the way to the CEO, "We're really a family. We treat each other with respect. We get to know people so that we really can support them and help mentor them."

However, Dana recognizes that the positive environment which he works to cultivate requires maintenance to ensure staff continue to treat residents with utmost respect throughout their time working with the organization. As

Dana explains, it goes beyond definitions written on a piece of paper, "The values part is literally articulating everyday respect or what we really mean by inclusion or choice. Any of those kinds of things that are so easy to lose."

This articulation comes with noticing the staff and how they treat the residents, as well as the vocabulary that they use even when residents are not present. By holding people accountable and praising positive practices, LSA has improved the group home experience for everyone involved.

Dana says oftentimes, they will see the same beautiful pattern:

> The classic example is a woman who's come from her parent's home, and has moved into her LSA house and within a couple of months her parents have come by to pick her up for the weekend, and she says, 'No, I don't want to go home, this is my home. I want to stay here, and I want to be with my friends.'

Although these changes can seem exceptional, Dana explains that in reality, "That's a transformation most everybody makes during their late teens and twenties. Living at home to living in their own home, and having their own relationships and work."

The truth is, parents will not always be able to take care of their child forever. However, LSA ensures that residents are not losing their family, but instead, adding more people to their family who want to help them live their best lives.

CHAPTER 9:

L'ARCHE

———

While the previous chapter showed the power of changing staff mentality while still maintaining caregiver/resident relationships, L'Arche, an international organization, shows that by breaking the barriers between caregivers and residents, both people with and without IDD can increase their quality of life.

Laura Goble had known about L'Arche's unique take on group housing since, in a college course on community psychology and community life, she read L'Arche founder Jean Venier's book, *Community and Growth*. In this story, she learned about how this Catholic philosopher opened his home in France to two men with severe disabilities in 1964 and lived alongside them even when virtually all people with disabilities were living in institutions.

In the book, Vernier describes developing a community with the individuals, and he defines community as "a place of belonging, a place where people are earthed and find their identity." To the present day, L'Arche has provided this type of community for both people with and without disabilities internationally, and Vernier remained an active disability advocate until his death in 2019.

L'Arche USA has communities in sixteen states which consist of one to eight group homes located within the same city. What makes the L'Arche community unique is its emphasis on the friendship between members of all neurodiversities rather than a DSP/resident relationship. In fact, the DSPs, or "assistants" in L'Arche lingo, live in the homes with the "core members" or individuals with IDD. Therefore, in addition to providing support to the residents, they also share their lives with them.

After reading Venier's book, Laura would not come in contact with L'Arche again until a couple years later, when her friend was an assistant at one of their group homes. Her friend asked Laura to "share a meal" with the members of the group home, a practice not unusual for L'Arche homes. As Laura explains:

A lot of times when we talk about L'Arche and try to explain to people what L'Arche is we say come to dinner, share a meal… so I went to a meal at a L'Arche community and that was my first time with L'Arche.

When a job opportunity to be director of Social Concerns at Gannon University took her to Eerie, Pennsylvania, in 2013, shortly after her experience at L'Arche, she was surprised to find out that the largest L'Arche community was located there. Because of the connection between the university and the community, "a lot of my work was accompanying people who were encountering L'Arche."

She helped students land jobs as assistants at the homes to gain invaluable experience working with people with IDD. She continued to direct others toward L'Arche until in 2016, a group of students needed a chaperone for their trip to an international L'Arche home in Hamilton, Ontario, for a week.

The trip was really serendipitous: "I wasn't originally scheduled to go with this group, somebody else was, but then they had an injury and weren't able to go with this student group. And I was the only person who had the skill set and also the passport, so I could go with this group at the last minute."

While remembering when she first set foot in the Canadian community, what comes to the front of her mind was the experience of, "Just sharing the daily rhythms of things like evening mealtime… and helping people with intellectual disabilities find their gifts." She saw assistants completing activities not uncommon in group homes: One person was helping a resident make sure they had everything they needed for work and seeing them out the door. In the afternoon, she saw other people helping prepare dinner for the residents. However, like the community she visited with her friend, after helping to make meals for the residents, the assistants were then sitting and sharing the meal with them.

They laughed and talked about the roses, thorns, and buds from their day when each person went around and gave one highlight, one struggle, and one thing they were looking forward to in the future. They were not just working for the core members, but they were developing relationships from which they could grow and enrich their lives. She said, "What was so cool to me was people with many different neurodiversities and cultural identities just sharing life in the same home, really helping each other."

Like in all L'Arche communities, even when some assistants were off duty, they often still had dinner with the house or would go to social events. There is always an invitation. In other words, the assistants had found a community that they valued beyond a paycheck.

When, at the end of the week, a community leader repeated the story of L'Arche's founding to Laura, she said, "I heard it in a new way." From when she first read the book in her college class, Jean Venier's story had always seemed intertwined with the Catholic faith. His descriptions of the program are often supported with biblical passages, and the values of giving to those less fortunate and growing in the process developed directly from the scripture. Knowing this background, Laura states, "I had always perceived L'Arche as a Catholic organization and a Catholic community, but I experienced that week with many different kinds of identities.... . they prayed in different ways and they shared spiritual practices in different ways." What stuck out to Laura when hearing the founding story was not the pious beliefs of the founder but that one of the first communities he helped to create was in India. This community had assistants and core members with both Christian and Hindu faiths living together. "Even though the community he originally built in France had a lot of Catholic practices... people from all kinds of faiths, practices and traditions were really moved by the mutuality that happens in L'Arche and the friendships that happen."

Within the year, Laura applied to take a position in the L'Arche community as interim eastern regional leader, and as of 2019, she holds the position of vice national leader of the American L'Arche program.

Looking back on Jean Venier first asking the two men with IDD to live with him and her own experience at the L'Arche home in Hamilton, Laura explains, "L'Arche has never been a program that serves people with intellectual disabilities, it's a program where people with many different neurodiversities serve each other."--

When I spoke to another representative at the L'Arche Boston North community in Massachusetts, Diana Giard, I asked for her explanation of how she felt people at L'Arche "serve each other." That was when she shared her L'Arche story with me.

She said she was talking to a friend, and that "I told her that I wanted to love people." Her friend then replied, "You know you should look into L'Arche." When she finished undergrad, unsure what the future would hold, she decided to apply to a L'Arche community in Cleveland: "I really didn't know what I was getting into when I went to Cleveland, so when I got there, there was an openness I had, not really knowing exactly what to expect, and it exceeded any expectations that I had." From there, "that experience was so transformative, that I brought that experience into my graduate program." After leaving L'Arche in 2010 to pursue her graduate degree, she returned to be the Spirituality and Outreach Coordinator at L'Arche Boston North in 2015.

**

These stories are just two examples of the profound effect L'Arche has on the people working there. By challenging the very nature of a DSP/resident relationship and instead offering friendships, L'Arche have become widely recognized as a top group home option on a national and international scale.

CHAPTER 10:

CHANGING THE HIRING POOL

———

Another key component of quality staff comes with the hiring process and determining the pool from which a group home chooses their staff. Even though my brother, Robb, is only 19 and has not moved out of our house, he has already had dozens of DSPs.

Finding quality staff is not an easy task. Although we now have really great DSPs who work with Robb, it has taken years of trial and error. One woman went to Las Vegas and never came back, and she was one of three direct support professionals who left the job without any warning, explanation, or contact afterward. Another time, my mom received a call from the police who said that they found my brother alone at the swing set in a park near our house even though he cannot be left unsupervised. My family still does not know what happened to the girl who stole our credit card before running away from the job.

These situations may seem like extreme caregiver short-comings. However, finding caregivers at all can be nearly impossible. The average turnover rate of caregivers or direct support professionals every year is 45 percent, and the average vacancy rate per year is 9 percent, which means that often group homes are sacrificing quality because of their immediate need for DSPs.[68] Target, a group home provider in Maryland, has implemented an innovative way to ensure that staff members are passionate about the work and have the correct educational background by changing the pool from which they hire.

TARGET COMMUNITY & EDUCATIONAL SERVICES, INC.

When Jeffery, Judy Woodruff's son, went in to have a routine surgery at 16, he had had relatively normal development up until that point. Although he was born with mild spina bifida and hydrocephalus, when recalling his childhood, Judy said, "He grew to be a little boy we couldn't even keep up with." He

---

68   "Staffing Shortages For Direct Support Professionals (DSPs)" *eWeb Schedule,* September 30, 2018.

swam, skied, and attended a rigorous school in their home, Washington, D.C. However, after a problem with the medical procedure, he left the surgery wheelchair bound, partially blind, and with brain damage. "He was never to be the same person, except on the inside."

Daily routines before the surgery were filled with school, homework, and sports, but now, "A normal day is like climbing a mountain. He has to have help with everything—getting out of bed, bathing." Even so, "Once we got over the shock of what had happened, we determined ourselves to make Jefferey's life as positive as possible."[69]

Judy is a trailblazer for women in the field of journalism, and her career has taken her from CNN to NBC to her current position as an anchorwoman and managing editor for PBS NewsHour. Because of her wide success as a newswoman, she had the resources to find the best options for her son. Jeffery transferred to Kennedy Krieger Institute, a world renowned school and research center on disabilities. There, they tried a wide range of treatments and therapies, and he also earned his high school diploma. Jeffery was then able to attend community college and later go away to college in South Carolina.

---

69 "As moderator of the first National Forum on Disability Issues today in Columbus, veteran broadcast journalist Judy Woodruff has a personal stake in the discussion." *The Columbus Dispatch,* July 26, 2008.

When Jeffery returned from college, he knew he wanted to live away from home, and so Judy again looked for the best option possible. By this time, Judy had even began expanding her work to help support disability journalism (for which she would later win the RespectAbility Excellence in Journalism award). In looking for the right housing option for Jeffery, she said:

> "We contacted about everyone we knew in our disability network, if you will. I contacted people at Kennedy Krieger Institute in Baltimore and a number of other organizations that I knew of in the in the DC area including national organizations."

In addition, one of Jeffery's caregivers who was getting his PhD in disability studies helped research companies to narrow down the ones that seemed to be the best fit. From the start, "The one that came back very quickly with very high recommendations was Target Community & Educational Services, Inc. located in Westminster, Maryland."

Target has eight groups homes integrated throughout Carroll County, Maryland, each of which has three to four residents and two caregivers. Upon looking through the homes, they are similar to many group homes in the county: Each resident has their own room with separate living arrangements for caregivers, and there are involved and well-trained staff.

However, Target remains the only program in the country where caregivers are actually part of a human services management master's program run through McDaniel College. In return for their services as the live-in caregivers at the home, the students receive 75 percent tuition reduction, free room and board, health-care benefits, a $22,000 stipend upon graduation, and hands-on experience to pursue a career in the nonprofit intellectual disability sector, the focus of their education. Designed by parents of adults with IDD, in 1983, from the start, Target communities have had the goal of reducing the turnover of caregivers and to help give experience to people who want to work with this population.[70]

By having the job as part of a master's program, all of the staff must complete at least two years at Target. They switch off having one student who has been in the house for one year and one new student every year, so there is always one person staying from one year to the next. Therefore, the transition between each person is as painless as possible.

This partnership with the college has allowed for quality care and lasting relationships between caregivers and residents of the homes. Courtney Tyler, a McDaniel College student who participated in the program said that the experience allowed her not only to gain invaluable experience, but also

---

70 Zirpoli, Tom. "Nonprofit View: McDaniel graduate program and Target Inc. work hand-in-hand." *Carroll County Times,* April 15, 2018.

"to have a job that I consider personally rewarding, working with others."

She recalled one time when a resident requested to hear Bob Dylan played in the car, and how excited she was at finding that they had similar taste in music: "It was just a really special moment for me because [the client] doesn't normally identify music. I was really excited about that."

Although she did not have experience working specifically with adults with IDD beforehand, she had a B.S. in social work like most of the caregivers in the program, and she quickly fell in love with the job. By having students newly emerging into the field and taking classes related to their job, Target has ensured that they have staff who are dedicated to and passionate about the work that they are doing.[71]

As Judy began narrowing down the search for her son, "We visited there, of course, and talked to the people there and just decided almost as soon as we had seen it, that this looked like a great option." Jeffery has remained in a Target home since 2010 and currently works at a Target-run vocational program.I know the amount of work it takes to take care of

---

71 Henderson, Nancy. "Right on Target: The Target Community and Educational Services Program Gives Graduate Students Crash Course in the Realities of Working with Individuals with Disabilities." *The Exceptional Parent*, September, 2008.

Jefferey and the other individuals, and it is jaw-dropping. It is extraordinary, the work they do," Woodruff wrote while reflecting on her experience with Target, "Especially as parents get older, they need a place that they can trust where their child will always get good, respectful care that gives them as much opportunity as possible."[72]

While Target is currently the only company in the country with this kind of partnership, Target CEO Dr. Tom Zirpoli has advised other organizations on how to start a program similar to the one they run and wants to help get this program started nationwide. They have proven its success. The next step is for more organizations to take the project on.

---

72 "The Science of Caregiving, Brining Voices Together." *The National Institute on Nursing Research.*

COMMUNITY RELATIONS INTRODUCTION

Throughout the early 1980s, the Governors' Planning Council on Developmental Disabilities in Illinois conducted over twenty studies nationwide to address concerns about the effects of the newly-developing group homes on the safety, stability, and property value of the surrounding neighborhoods. All of these studies showed that group homes had no effect on these factors within communities.[73] However,

---

73 Lauber, Daniel. "Impacts on the Surrounding Neighborhood of Group Homes for Persons With Developmental Disabilities." *Governor's Planning Council on Developmental Disabilities,* September 1896.

for many years to come, homeowners continued to oppose group homes in their communities.

In a New York Times article written in 1995, over ten years after the studies were conducted in Illinois, the headline reads "For Group Homes, No Easy Victories; Year After Year, Communities Rebuff the Mentally Retarded." The article interviewed a member of a neighborhood in Queens who was fighting to close a group home. The homeowner initially claimed, "People are fearful of the home and what it could do to their property values," but he goes on to say, "People are fearful living in Queens because it has become a dumping ground for all of New York City." Although many people masked their dislike for group homes with unfounded price arguments, oftentimes their resentment was, in reality, ableism.[74]

In 2018, in an interview with NPR, Patty Rabe, a parent of an adult with IDD, states that even in current times, "When people with disabilities want to come into a neighborhood, there's a lot of pushback, and the people are afraid."[75] While it seems like an issue which should have been resolved years ago, I was not surprised at hearing about people's fight against

---

74 Holloway, Lynette. "For Group Homes, No Easy Victories; Year After Year, Communities Rebuff the Mentally Retarded." *The New York Times,* July 18, 1995.

75 Tribou, Doug. "Creating A Community For People With Developmental Disabilities." *NPR,* February 4, 2018.

group homes in their community. Even going to the movies or out to dinner, my family has endured complaints from other customers, and we are only there for a couple of hours.

To combat stigmatism, increased community engagement has become an emphasis in group homes throughout the country, and many homes are taking matters into their own hands and developing unique community connections to enhance the quality of community relations. This section will have three chapters on intentional communities, mixed-use communities, and how group homes can connect with their community and even save funds while doing so. These examples are all original approaches not only on how to encourage positive community ties but also how to utilize the surrounding communities. Similar to organizations mentioned in previous chapters, many of these organizations also incorporate new approaches to design, staff, and funding.

CHAPTER 11:

INTENTIONAL COMMUNITIES

The Fellowship for Intentional Communities defines Intentional Communities as "a group of people who live together or share common facilities and who regularly associate with each other on the basis of explicit common values."[76] For decades, people have designed intentional communities for adults with IDD where they can live alongside neighbors who know and embrace the IDD community.

While these communities have faced barriers to funding due to fear of causing unnecessary isolation and segregation of people with IDD, advocacy across the country has helped

---

76 "About The Foundation for Intentional Community." *Foundation for Intentional Community.*

promote this model and it has gained support nationwide (see Chapter 4: Choice for more information).[77]

This chapter describes two intentional communities, each of which is unique based on its residents. The places discussed in this chapter are both examples of co-housing models, a type of intentional community where neighborhoods have residents with and without IDD who choose to live there and want to build relationships with their neighbors.

BUILDING OHANA

When I spoke with, Deborah Finck, the executive director and co-founder of Building Ohana, an intentional community in Spokane, Washington, she said that her primary motivation to create the community came from her son, Jonathan, who has IDD. As she began to brainstorm for his future and look at potential living options,

> I wasn't so much looking for housing options as an inclusive community where Jonathan could live a life of purpose and connection... What I saw around me was so much isolation based on fragmented service models and very little engagement within

---

77 "Housing Options for Individuals with Disabilities: Intentional Communities." *M&L Special Needs Planning,* May 2, 2013.

neighborhoods and communities for people with developmental disabilities.

Ultimately, Building Ohana is trying to develop what other group homes claim to develop: true connections in the community.

In 2012, Deborah along with other families began developing the plan for Building Ohana. They named the company "ohana" because the word means family in Hawaiian (blood or non-blood related), and they believe that their community should be a family with strong bonds between all the residents.

In order to ensure that community members are engaging with one another, Building Ohana, the nonprofit, will provide activities in which everyone can participate.

> The common house, the heart of OHANA, will exist as a meeting place and a second home to provide a space for residents to engage at many levels, in small groups and as an entire community. Most of our green spaces, urban gardens, and recreational areas will be designed for shared experiences.

As part of their housing plan, they ensure that the communities are not a one-size-fits-all model: "As it will be a mixed-tenure community, there will be many options to suit diverse groups." This model means that there may be individuals with IDD who are living in group homes while others who require fewer supports may live alone. However, everyone will be supported by the surrounding community. The community in total will include 120 residents with and without disabilities.

Also, the people who plan to join the Ohana community do so before the community is built so that they can be a part of the process of its development:

> All along we have invited the community to get involved with Building Ohana. By the time our community is on the ground, our residents will have been part of its design and development, and through our Pathways to Residency program, will have determined how they will best engage with Ohana. Some will purchase homes, others will rent or help their loved ones to move into a supported home within the community.

This means that once the community opens, its residents will already have formed relationships to ensure its success.

As of 2019, Building Ohana is in negotiation for 7.7 acres of land in the Spokane area located within a master-planned community development, allowing connections to the broader community and access to nearby rivers and trails. From there, they already have the business plan laid out:

If we secure this property, our financial and site plans are ready to be implemented over the course of the next eighteen months, with a community-based design process that will include stakeholders and potential residents into the creation of Ohana Village. In short, we are in predevelopment, and it all depends on securing our property within the next several months—we are at this point quite hopeful. Our goal at this point is to be on the ground and occupied by fall of 2021.

THREE OAKS COMMUNITIES

The goal of Building Ohana is extremely local. The families are building their community to meet their own needs while at the same time connecting with the other families in the neighborhood. In the development of an intentional community in Michigan, however, another developer was asking: "How can the process be expanded? How can we create a model that can be duplicated in other communities to address the needs of individuals with IDD and their families throughout the United States and beyond?"

In Saline, Michigan, the idea for the intentional community started similarly to that in Spokane. A group of Saline families contacted local real estate developer Bill Godfrey about building housing for their adult children with IDD.

Bill knew firsthand the potential this model had. His grandparents began the process of looking for housing options for his uncle Bruce who had intellectual disabilities in the 1980s. Although Bruce was high functioning, he needed a more structured living arrangement. "He was a little kid. He was probably an 8-year-old in an 80-year-old body when he finally passed away last year, and he was a great person." The option his grandparents finally found was a house located about an hour away from their home. "He had to kind of start a brand new life by himself, which he did, because he was just a very strong character and big personality. But it would have been so much better if he could have just stayed closer to home by his family and friends. When he came home to visit, I just remember thinking how difficult it was for him to live so far from his family and hometown."

Long before co-founding Three Oaks Communities, Bill entered the residential and commercial real estate business, a field seemingly unrelated to the IDD community: "We started out acquiring and renovating historic homes into graduate student housing on the University of Michigan campus. We did that for ten years and then sold all of those properties. That was chapter one, providing nice apartments for graduate students near the University of

Michigan central campus."Chapter two was acquiring, renovating, and managing large office buildings in Grand Rapids, Michigan. When describing the work, Bill states, "It was a very commercial business, with customers such as banks, law firms, accounting firms, hospitals, foundations, government agencies, restaurants, and other local businesses, which is very different from building homes for sale to adults with IDD, their families, and the general public." By 2015, they had sold most of their commercial real estate portfolio, but Bill and his partner were ready to take on something new. Serendipitously, as chapter two was concluding, the Saline families contacted Bill about building IDD housing, and the idea for chapter three began to emerge.

Bill began to research IDD housing options throughout the country and realized that although there were some very exciting IDD housing models being developed in other parts of the country, there wasn't a for-profit model that integrated new construction homes for sale to adults with IDD and their families with new construction homes for sale to the general public. Thereafter, the idea for building inclusive neighborhoods was born, and Bill and his partners knew the idea had great potential. "As we dug into it, we realized there is huge and unmet demand for IDD housing throughout the country, so we decided to turn the idea into a business model."

The Saline families embraced the idea and joined Three Oaks in the planning phase for their first inclusive neighborhood, Maple Oaks. Although Three Oaks did not have any experience building homes for adults with IDD, they found that their lack of preconceived notions could often work as an advantage.

We would go to meetings, and the parents would disagree about what type of housing should be built. I thought to myself, "The only way this will ever work is if we start with a blank canvas and customize the homes." We began to meet with families and asked them to tell us what they wanted. "We'll try to give it to you," was our response. People wanted different things, but they didn't argue because they were going to get exactly what they wanted.

Throughout my interview with Bill, he emphasized the fact that every home will look different:

> Homebuyers with IDD are so unique, just like market rate homebuyers. All buyers have lots of different needs and preferences. You can't prescribe one size; one size does not fit all.

Not all of the requests seemed like textbook examples of important features in IDD homes either. Bill was often surprised by what the homeowner wanted. When speaking to one parent about what he envisioned for the home of his 19-year-old son who would be moving into the community, he said, "One of the things that is very comforting to him is to have a hanging chair, that he can sit in and swing around. It's soothing to him." Three Oaks put extra blocking into the ceiling to support two hanging chairs in his condominium, one in his bedroom and one in the living room.

Other designs, rather than focusing on the clients' different abilities or needs, are solely based on the clients' interests. For example, if a customer has a drum set and likes to play drums, Three Oaks can add additional soundproofing.

However, a couple of patterns did start to emerge. Many families' requests centered around personal care items:

Something that's kind of nuts and bolts is laundry machines in the bathroom. Personal care is a big challenge for some of our adult customers with IDD, so putting the shower in the bathtub, and the toilet and laundry sheets all in one room makes a ton of sense. In general, you would not see that in a typical home.

Three Oaks plans to use the information provided from the IDD home customization process at Maple Oaks to customize homes for future customers. "We're going to keep accumulating data that will be useful to the families going forward in all of our future plans."

In total, Maple Oaks includes eight condominiums for adults with IDD as well as sixteen townhomes and ten single-family homes for the general public. The homebuyers with IDD, their families, and the general public thoroughly supported the idea of living in an inclusive neighborhood; all of the homes at Maple Oaks were pre-sold within eighteen months, including two homes that were purchased by parents who wanted to live across the street from their adult children with IDD. Bill was not surprised. "In every one of these neighborhoods, there are going to be a few super moms and dads who are committed to making sure their sons and daughters make a successful transition to more independent living, that's a given."

When Three Oaks began planning Maple Oaks, they decided that approximately 25 percent of the homes should be sold to adults with IDD to ensure critical mass to attract caregiving services because they need only provide services to a single location instead of multiple locations.

The presence of caregiving services also made the neighborhood attractive to families with younger children with IDD. "They want to be in the neighborhood because it's inclusive and welcoming and people "get it." And the services are there."

To further support families in the process, Three Oaks also organized training for the parents of homebuyers with IDD at Maple Oaks. "In our travels, we met an excellent organization in Evanston, Illinois, called Center for Independent Futures." Center for Independent Futures' mission is to help adults with IDD and their families develop the skills that are necessary for an adult with IDD to live as independently as possible. "We were so impressed with Center for Independent Futures' model that we decided to send all of the parents who are buying homes for their loved ones with IDD at Maple Oaks to a three-day workshop at Center for Independent Futures' location in Evanston, Illinois." (See Chapter 3: Creating a Home for more information on Center for Independent Futures)

For the overall structure of Maple Oaks, there will be two fourplex buildings in the neighborhood with condominiums that are attached but still provide the homeowner with their own space that has a separate legal description and tax identification number, which are important for financing and private property rights. The base plan for all of the condos includes two bedrooms and one bathroom with a large living room and kitchen/dining area. Some of the families have customized the units to include two bedrooms and two bathrooms. The Maple Oaks condominium floor plans allow residents to have live-in caregivers, roommates, or a place for their parents and siblings to stay when they visit.

The base price for a two-bedroom condominium in Maple Oaks was $180,0000. Since their first offering, Three Oaks has designed other fourplexes for future projects; some at a lower price point to make them more affordable for families on limited budgets. Bill noted that "to use an overused analogy, we will be offering Chevys as well as Cadillacs for our future projects."

As they talked to potential homebuyers and their families, Three Oaks also learned that some adults who required fewer supports want a home design that offers a little more independence with some supervision. As a result, they created a design for "cottages." There are three or four cottages around a caregiver office building. The entire layout is then integrated into the overall neighborhood.

To be able to adjust the format as they begin developing communities, Three Oaks also created the concept of "flex areas," a "site plan within a site plan" that they will continue to develop and utilize:

> In our next project, for example, the city approved us
> having just two large open areas that we designated
> as flex areas that we can build. This is an exciting
> concept because it gives us the flexibility to provide
> a variety of custom homes and floor plans tailored
> to the homebuyers' needs.

Even though Three Oaks plans to scale up and build more inclusive neighborhoods in Michigan and other parts of the country, Bill acknowledges that current demand greatly exceeds the potential supply:

> There is a huge need out there for this. It's impossible to meet it all, but what we're hoping to do and what happens a lot of times is that you can do these smaller demonstration projects, so that people will say, wow, this is how they did it, I can do it in my hometown.

In addition to developing its own projects, Three Oaks hopes to eventually partner with other housing groups and developers around the country who would like to create inclusive neighborhoods with them. The development of an inclusive neighborhood is not a trivial undertaking. Bill admits "It's overwhelming at times.... . I've been in real estate for nearly thirty years and I can't recall any project that was as complex as building an inclusive neighborhood on vacant land."

After NPR Morning Edition ran a story on Maple Oaks in early 2018, Three Oaks was approached by a number of different housing groups for people with IDD from around the country who wanted to know how they could build their own inclusive neighborhoods. Bill's advice to them:

Before you begin the process, put a team together that includes a builder, a broker, and a banker. With a good team in place, you will be we ready to start the process. Although we are not ready to be part of that process yet, we hope to be so in the near future.

For the future, the possibilities are endless. After committing to the Maple Oaks project, Bill says that: "All of a sudden, all these things start to come into view that we didn't see before, because we hadn't made the commitment to do it yet. It's a fascinating thing that happens when you commit yourself to something that you think is going to work, but you're not sure. And then all of a sudden, it's like, wow, all these amazing possibilities start to emerge with an inclusive neighborhood, and you can be overwhelmed by all of it. We are constantly reminding ourselves to focus on the basics of building homes and helping families organize caregiving services for adults with IDD first. That's the most important thing. There are many potential enhancements to our inclusive neighborhood model, but most of them can wait until later."

For example, the day before I spoke to Bill, he told me that while at a birthday party, "I ran into a person who works next door to our office in Saline. She works for an autonomous vehicle company called Navya." After asking her about Navya and the autonomous vehicles they manufacture, Bill learned that the vehicles are already in use on the University of Michigan campus and other areas around the world. Although that was just the first conversation, Bill could see the possibilities these vehicles could offer in his communities:

> That technology could be huge for adults with IDD in the future because transportation is one of the biggest challenges for adults with IDD… to get out of the house, go to the store, get groceries, go to the pharmacy or the movies, etc.

Looking forward to completing Maple Oaks in 2020 and beginning new projects, Bill says:It was the best thing we ever did. By taking that leap of faith, we had enough. We didn't have everything in place, but we had enough to prove that building an affordable and inclusive neighborhood can work for homebuyers with IDD, their families, the general public, and the larger community.

CHAPTER 12:

MIXED-USE
COMMUNITIES

———

A mixed-use community is a community where individuals with intellectual and developmental disabilities can find residential services, jobs, and recreational opportunities all in one place. These types of communities represent a growing movement to help create sustainable housing opportunities in which people with and without IDD can live.

Many of these communities which arise throughout the country may have group homes, but some also offer independent housing options or apartment complexes. The following chapter will discuss Camphill Village, which offers group homes within their community along with LTO Ventures whose model includes a variety of housing options. While the original Camphill Village in England started in 1939, and the LTO Ventures model is currently developing its first community, both were founded with the goal of improving the lives of people with IDD through creating sustainable communities.

CAMPHILL VILLAGE

When asked to sum up Camphill Village Copake, located in New York, associate director of Development, Richard Neal says:

> The culture in Camphill Village is based on what we call the three essentials of Camphill—the first essential is a recognition that in every human being regardless of any outer manifestations of limitation or disability resides an eternal human healthy spirit. The second essential is that every human being has the right and I would say the responsibility to develop and learn and grow. The third essential is a continuous striving to create community to bring people together so that they can do more together than any one of them could have managed to do alone.

Since Camphill Village Copake's founding in 1961, there have been a total of fifteen villages created in North America, all of which share the same model. Today Camphill

Village Copake itself has grown into a 600-acre community of 240 people, about half of whom have developmental disabilities. However, the Camphill essentials still remain the basis of the community.When Susan Williams first began the process of looking for her son Tony's living situation around 2007, she had no idea what the future would hold. Her son is fairly nonverbal and had been diagnosed with autism, and she knew that in the future she would need to find him a job, activities, a home, and other things to help him develop a fulfilling life: "You just begin to wonder, what's next?" It was around this time that she found Camphill Copake, and she says, "I never thought a place like this existed."

Although Camphill maintains the group home style of having less than six individuals with disabilities living together in homes in integrated communities, unlike other group homes, the entire Camphill community is made up of people who have chosen to live and work there. The people without IDD include families, couples, and single individuals. Some of these individuals are volunteering for a year while some have made the location their home, and all of them also work in the community.

After his move to Camphill, Tony became a woodworker, and he has not only loved the community but experienced growth while in it: "He's a lot calmer than he's ever been. He seems to really respond to this slower rhythm and this connection with nature and community."[78]

Individuals in group homes must also have access to day or vocational programs for activities since they can no longer take part in the public school system. With Camphill Village, all of these services can be accessed in one place. Jean-David, a staff member at Camphill explains their set-up, stating: "Work is a very important thing for any human being, here everyone is called on to contribute to work even if a person can't do much because any contribution is expression of one's belonging to a group of human beings."[79]

They have separated the jobs into eleven different options for the residents living there. Every job helps to contribute to the sustainability of the community. For example, the village includes a working farm with sheep, cows, and pigs, and individuals working in the farm wake up before sunrise to milk the cows and take them out into the pasture. This farm, along with their gardens, are dedicated to biodynamic agriculture, which means that they minimize the amount of waste which they create. The food given to the animals will

---

78 "Camphill Village Copake, New York." *The Camphill Village Copake Foundation,* June 3, 2013.

79 "Let Each Light Shine: A Portrait of Camphill Village." *The Camphill Village Copake Foundation,* July 6, 2016.

be scraps from the gardens, and they use the garden and the produce to cook their meals.

Individuals can work in other settings including a "weavery," a "book bindery," a candle-shop, and a stained-glass studio. All of the goods which they create are then sold by other individuals at a store on-site for an extra stream of income into the community. Because both individuals with and without disabilities work together, it creates a stronger bond between the staff and the people with IDD in the community. Jean-David goes on to describe his role in the community: "The fact that the work I do is not for myself but for the whole really makes me feel that I am in a link with others, and that is really what our community is resting on."

By ensuring that everyone in the community plays an integral part in contributing to its sustainability, Camphill Copake has created a culture in which people with IDD are not burdens to society but instead valued parts of their community. Therefore, the relationships that form between individuals with and without IDD do not happen artificially. They are all working in the same jobs for a common purpose.

LTO VENTURES

Mark Olson, an advocate for community choice, became an expert on housing when he was ascertaining what his daughter was showing him were her needs, desires, and opportunities for a meaningful life (see *Community Choice* for more information). He had visited settings throughout the country, yet he still had not found an option which ideally suited her needs. However, while sitting in his office:

> I had kind of an epiphany one day, and it was just one of those days where I filled my head with so much information, and I took the attitude alright if she could talk to me what would she tell me would be her ideal life when I'm not around?

It was from there that he first developed what he dubbed the "live/work/play concept."

- He said at first he thought, "She's got to **live**. I am highly doubtful that government funding will ever become available to her, so I had to figure out where the money is going to come from. Some is obviously going to come from me, but can she work?"
- That is when he started thinking about her potentially having a job, "We all like to **work**. Especially if it's doing things that we like to do. It's where you make friendships, it's where you gain a lot of esteem and it keeps your brain working all day. So alright, that's the work part."
- Finally, he thought of the last leg of his housing vision for Lindsay: "She's very social. She likes to be around people,

she may not engage with them, but she really likes to be around them. So, I said, 'Okay, so that's kind of the **play** social aspect of it.'"

He states that the concept and the term, "It's not new. There are a million people who use live/work/play or live/work/worship, or live/work/play/worship or live/work/learn or live/learn/play. There are all sorts of combinations of that. I decided I am going to make live/work/play our thing."

From there, he began to address his housing vision with the question, "What are the problems that I need to solve for her?" He considered his daughter and her individual needs: "She's four and a half feet tall, fully grown. She doesn't speak, read, or write. She's got autism, some intellectual disability, epilepsy, polycystic ovarian syndrome.... . So medications are always going to be part of her life. But she doesn't necessarily have to be tethered to a DSP, a direct support professional, 24/7."

That was what led him to a series of questions about the different problems he wanted to solve:

- "How do I create an environment where she can be as independent as possible but as safe as possible? She loves walking out the front door, going over to the next door, and knocking on the door or just walking in the house, so how do I create an environment where that's okay?"

- "Is it big group homes, is it an apartment building, is it little homes?" At the time, he already had an idea in mind for his daughter and her ideal housing option which he dubbed "small homes." In this home, Lindsay could have her own space, or she could share the home with an individual without disabilities to help her out.

As he continued to develop the model for his daughter, he began to think about problems for many people with IDD. One that immediately came to mind was obesity and weight management. With that issue in mind, he asked himself the question, "How do I create a physical environment where you have to get out, walk around and get fresh air and exercise?" As a solution, he considered a pedestrian-oriented community: "You put all the cars on the outside, leave all the people on the inside, like a college quad."

Another aspect he considered was impact: "How big does it need to be? We've got 5 million adults in the United States with intellectual and developmental disabilities, a million of them live with caregivers, age 60 or older, you know, there's a huge wave coming." He felt that building a community for just five people did not seem big enough to address the problem, but building something for hundreds of people would be too big to ensure quality care to all residents. "That's where it kind of settled on one hundred or 120."

As he more fully developed how the "live" aspect of the community would work, he then began to think about how they could incorporate the job aspect.

When considering his daughter, he knew that "her disabilities and lack of communication skills are not going to make it possible for her to work in a regular workplace at a Walmart or a law firm or a hospital, without being tethered to somebody the entire time." That is why the idea of social enterprises appealed to Mark. In his research on different organizations serving the community of people with IDD, in Chapel Hill, North Carolina, Mark had found a social micro-enterprise center for individuals with IDD called Extraordinary Ventures which showed how companies with supported jobs could also be successful.

He then went on to develop a preliminary idea for how the play aspect of the community would work. He began envisioning a social center, similar to intentional communities which he called a "full blown" community center: "A gym and a pool, and a music room where you play instruments or learn instruments, a video game room, a cafe... sort of a true community center." He envisions both people in the wider community and residents with IDD in the community center, but unlike community centers in neurotypical communities, "all the programming, and all the resources are oriented toward the individuals with disabilities.... The analogy I use is wheelchair basketball. Anybody can play wheelchair basketball, you just have to be in a wheelchair, just like everybody else in a wheelchair. If you fall over, you have got to get up like everybody else gets up, so it levels the playing field."

Similar to the intentional communities discussed in the previous chapter, because the community center is targeted towards people with IDD, that means that people without IDD: "They're going to come in with the right attitude.... . I'm not about forced integration."

After developing the preliminary live/work/play, he then went on to think about the overall structure of the community, and determined:

> It would be really cool if it was all on one campus, like you could walk to work if you wanted, or if you wanted to have a job outside the community, you could just get on transportation and go to it.

He imagines that when his daughter gets up in the morning, she can walk to work on the property: "When she's done she might think I don't want to go home right now. I want to go hang out at the Community Center, see who's here, watch kids doing silly things, get a snack." Therefore, she will have more opportunities to make choices while living in the community.

Thinking about the center, he continued to think of more and more features: "There's also an idea that the campus would include a dining facility, because she can't work a stove or a microwave, but she likes hot food, just like we all do, so we want to have it available. She knows how to walk down a lunch line and pick out the things she wants to eat."

As Mark began developing the business plan for his model, he began to hone in on the key factor in the success of any business, the finances. "I had to think about well, how do we pay for all this? How do the residents pay for this?"

Government funding never seemed like a viable option to Mark, because for individuals to get community waivers to pay for the community, "You could be on the waitlist to get funding to pay for your support to live in the community, but you can't wait on that list for fourteen or fifteen years."

From there, Mark began to think about how the community itself could promote sustainable practice or "design as a way to reduce cost." What he came up with was the idea that, "If I make it a neurodiverse community, where 75 percent of the residents are adults with disabilities, but 25 percent are adults without disabilities. Now I've intentionally created natural support."

While they would not be the direct support professionals that many residents with IDD would also need, he envisions that these were the kind of people who would naturally look after their neighbor. "I'm thinking like, retired teachers, retired nurses, retired clergy, people who have giving in their DNA, or graduate students in disability studies programs who want to live in an immersive experience, or individuals or couples who are just those people in the world who when they were age six, were going, 'I'm going to join the Peace Corps.' That's just the way they're wired."

He envisions some of these individuals living in his small homes clustered around other people with IDD:

> You have these beautiful front porches or shared front porches, so that, people living close to each other, are very aware of each other. The little sidewalks, from the front of the homes all kind of empty out into a space, right in front of all like eight homes. If you put eight homes together, two of them are going to be occupied by people without disabilities, six of them are going to be occupied by people with disabilities.

By having these people all in such close proximity, "Somebody's always going to know if they've seen their neighbor. Somebody is paying attention."

Another key benefit of an intentional design like this is you improve the service utilization and cost-effectiveness of paid supports, reducing the amount of funding needed. "If you do have paid staff that need to come in and spend some time with individuals, you could have one person almost taking care of, say, four to six people because everything is localized."

Cost-reduction also comes into play with the social micro-enterprise center in the community. Although some people may only be able to work ten hours a week while others can work thirty, many people can still contribute to a job. All of the work opportunities which Mark envisions are meant to be profitable: "They make real things they charge real money for, and they get paid real money, and they pay real taxes."

Also, adults with disabilities would be paired with adults without disabilities in integrated teams which creates friendships and turns adults without disabilities into advocates informed by their actual experiences. Not only does the process provide a meaningful experience for all individuals involved, but Mark explains,

> Those profits go back into the community, the campus community and help underwrite the costs of operating, so now you've reduced the cost of operating. Also, you've created more income for the

residents who were there, and you've taken some of the burden off of the parents, and you're not reliant on government funding.

When Mark began to put this plan in motion, he continued his research: "I'm traveling to visit settings and attending conferences, looking for best practices and innovative ideas to incorporate into my design." He said a friend came up to him and said, "Well, all right, you have an idea, how are you going to make it happen?"

He started by forming a nonprofit and inviting people to join the board. He chose people who he thought understood and were committed to the issue. From there he continued to get advice on how to develop the product. The board members told him to write the model down, and Mark wrote model describing the property. They then told him to create a website, so people could learn about the model. In turn, "I built a website, and a Facebook page, and a Twitter page. And I kept researching. I kept going around and visiting places."

When determining where to first try creating the model, he assumed he would spearhead the project where he was living, in Henderson, Nevada, located in the Las Vegas Valley. However, when he looked at the prices, "Land in Las Vegas was a half a million dollars an acre, and I'm a 20-acre design. $10 million was just an insurmountable number."

Despite the problems with creating the community in Nevada, he continued the conversation and continued to give presentations on the issues. Then in 2015, an organization in Cincinnati that wanted to build an IDD living model expressed interest in building the design, and he began consulting them the following year. Now, the LTO Ventures live/work/play model is taking shape in Cincinnati with the organization Ken Anderson Alliance.

Although he started the work with the organization in Cincinnati as a consultant, they eventually hired him as the executive director, and he moved to Ohio to drive the development of the property. They decided to piece the program together by starting the Play and Work programs before the location was built:

> What we found in making the community a reality is that as an organization, you want to be serving adults with disabilities as quickly as you can. First of all, it's a credibility issue. Second of all, it's the right thing to do, because there's an incredible need. Third, you're building your base of supporters.

The team decided to start with the play aspect of the community, and in 2017, they opened a small group social outings program where four to eight adults with disabilities and a couple of staff and volunteers go, "Do what everybody else does—you go to ball games. You go to movies, to dinner and shopping. You volunteer." They have continued to develop the program, and as of 2019, it serves 175 people, and every month they have twenty-five outings.

After getting that program up and running in 2018, they connected with another nonprofit, O2 Urban Farms and Vineyard Westside church to create an aquaponics farm. "It's meant to employ adults with disabilities, and we've got a bunch of adults working over there right now." Although they cannot actually move the operation to the live location, when it is built, they plan to develop a new aquaponics operation with the company on the campus. Like the first program, "as a proof of concept, it's been very successful."

Since these programs have been developed, Ken Anderson Alliance bought twenty-two acres of land in Cincinnati to begin the process of building the live community whose model is based off of Mark's original design. As of this writing in 2019, it is about to break ground.

Mark has since transitioned out of his official role with the Ken Anderson Alliance and currently lives in Texas, where he plans to begin the process of creating another LTO Ventures model. He hopes to continue raising awareness about the model, so it can be developed in different areas throughout the country.

CHAPTER 13

FUNDING AND COMMUNITY

———

While it would take hundreds of additional pages to go through all of the complexities and problems with funding in every state on both the organization and family sides, below are innovative ways two organizations are maximizing their funds while also developing connections within the communities.

FLYING COLORS OF SUCCESS, INC.

When I first spoke to the CEO of Flying Colors of Success, Michael Hardesty, I was already aware of the amazing community in which the organization is located which I have already mentioned multiple times in this book. Carroll

County, Maryland holds the Ivy League of group homes and day programs.

Individuals with IDD living in Carroll County have direct support as high school students transitioning into community living. The local organizations examine each student's profile and help to find them a viable opportunity, eliminating the stress of finding the appropriate programs and funding on their own. This is one of the only counties to do so nationwide. When I asked how the community figured out this system, Michael stated, "The spirit of cooperation in the whole nonprofit sector in Carroll County is really pretty amazing."

From its start in 1991, Flying Colors has worked to develop relationships with the other local group home providers in order for all of them to be successful. Every month the CEOs meet and discuss ways to collaborate and share resources. For example, the state government has mandatory training requirements for individuals with IDD for which the organizations must pay, but by training staff from different organizations in the same session, the companies can share the cost. This idea seems so simple, yet in most areas, organizations remain separated. Mike explained the problem stating:

> We're all sort of doing the same thing.... We're
> still competing for resources. We're competing for

funding. We're competing for fundraised dollars. We're competing for supplemental money from county or state government.

Because the government only has a set amount they provide in each county, money they gain may come at the expense of other organizations. He says that's why, when people consider group housing providers as a way to make money, "you can look at another organization as competition because there's only so many slices you can get out of a pie, and everybody wants to get the biggest slice they can." What makes the most difference in Carroll County, and what has fueled their relationship is their motive:

> If you can get people to do things, for the common good of the individuals they are serving, I think that's where it's at. And I think that's historically been a good thing here in Carroll County. Carroll County has a lot of different human service agencies, and they all work well together. It's really a special place to work.

This cooperation extends to other organizations throughout the county, which has allowed for the creation of some amazing programs. For example, a senior inclusion program allows older men and women with IDD to go to a local senior center and participate in activities with the residents there.

As many people with disabilities age and face increased physical challenges, they have fewer community activities available to them. This program creates a fun activity while also promoting community engagement. Although it has been in existence for over twenty years, still no other county in Maryland has anything similar in place.

In another progressive program, a special populations group consisting of people from nursing homes, hospitals, and assisted living for elderly people with IDD get together every month to study disaster planning. The day I spoke with Mike, the group was engaged in an active shooter training class. This program, in addition to promoting community connection, also makes sure that in emergency situations residents are prepared, making the homes safer as a whole.

Even though there are limited resources for which group home organizations must compete, Flying Colors of Success shows that there is so much more that can be done through cooperation rather than competition. Ultimately, these connections can improve the quality of life of residents as a whole.

L'ARCHE BOSTON NORTH

Another practice which has developed among group homes to find an additional sources of cash flow is micro-enterprises.

This concept has increased in popularity throughout the country, and both the Building Ohana intentional community and LTO Ventures envision implementing the practice in their operations.

L'Arche Boston North has begun putting the concept into practice with—surprisingly—a hummus business. This idea demonstrates how the possibilities for a business can expand beyond being solely an income source but also a tool for community engagement and job opportunities.

When the L'Arche Boston North's community leader wanted to involve members of their homes in the community farmers market, she knew the item they would want to sell from the start: hummus. "It all started because we had this Taste of Spring event," explained the community's Spirituality and Outreach Coordinator Diana Giard. "We would have hundreds of people, and every year, Emma made this hummus."

People at the event constantly approached the leaders to ask, "How do we get this hummus? Where can we buy this?" However, up until 2017, the answer had always been that it was just something they had for the event, and it was not for sale. That is until the community leader approached Emma, an assistant at the home, about getting a team together to make the hummus for the local farmers market.

In preparation for the first year they would be at the market, the community went through the process of certifying two of the kitchens, so that the hummus could be produced within the actual homes. Looking back on that summer, "it was pretty intense," Diana recalls. "It was primarily Emma who was making the hummus, and the core members who were helping out."

Even so, as the first year of the farmers market came to a close, the hummus allowed for increased community involvement and a small profit as well: "It was pretty cool to see how much it shot up in the first year."

However, going into the second year, Emma decided to decrease their participation in the event to once every two weeks instead of every week and to increase resident involvement by having residents help at every step of the process. "It was definitely an amazing collaborative effort," Diana said.

Six weeks before the second farmers market, the residents helped to plan the different flavors, which included everything from sweet potato paprika to sriracha and roasted red pepper, and they then developed a list of the necessary ingredients. Another group would then go to the store to buy the ingredients, and others would make the labels to put onto the hummus jars for sale. Finally, a group of two core members and one assistant, dubbed the "Tiki Dream

Team" or "Garbanzo Gang," made the hummus with Emma supervising as the head chef.

When the farmers market finally arrived, other groups of core members and assistants helped to sell the hummus, gaining first hand interactions with members of the surrounding community. The second year, the hummus continued to be a huge success as people asked, "Can we order it in bulk? Where can I find this in the wintertime?"

As the sale of hummus at the summer farmer's market continues, the assistants brainstorm ways to increase the hummus production in the future, including potentially creating a day program that could make hummus year-round. Even though grants and funding would need to be considered in the process of developing these larger programs, Diana is optimistic about the hummus ventures' potential: "We have something that we know is lucrative; something that would give us a start."

All of the funds from the hummus social enterprise have gone back into the company, and although the organization did not specify how funds from their social enterprise would be delegated, Diana states that for organizations like L'Arche: "A lot of times, I think these social enterprises help to fund things that help to maintain quality of life whenever the rest of their basic needs are met by government funding."

The opportunities these additional programs provide could depend on the person utilizing them and their interest. For example, maybe it is "a core member who really can't afford a lesson but really would love to take an art class or music lessons, or swimming or a personal trainer, or those types of things where they really want to have an opportunity to do something." The funding could even be provided for something like a vacation because as Diana explains, "A lot of people think, 'oh, well, a vacation that's a luxury,' but all of us get to go on some type of vacation at some point in time."

Ultimately, the future impact of the hummus social enterprise on different programs in L'Arche Boston North is not yet known. But it is a hopeful example of how the development of social enterprises can provide opportunities for community involvement and increased funding opportunities for group homes.

WHAT'S NEXT?

———

We have now looked at over sixteen different organizations which have developed innovative approaches to housing across the nation ranging from small changes in technique to large-scale projects. Whew! All of the different types of innovation may seem overwhelming, and they beg the question, "What's Next?"

I wish I could conclude this story with a big, innovative action that my family took to create the perfect housing option for Robb implementing the different practices discussed. However, my family, like so many others, is still in a state of uncertainty as to what will happen. In the meantime, we continue to add Robb's name to waiting lists, tour housing options, talk to other parents, and ask tons and tons of questions. After doing this research, a conclusion seemed unreasonable because even the "What's Next?" is still unclear. The housing crisis is still very real for my family and many others.

Even so, while we have not taken a big innovative step to create Robb's ideal housing solution (yet), as Robb continues to walk on the pathway to housing, the vision I have for my brother's future has changed continuously over the course of writing this book. I always knew that I wanted Robb to have a design, staff, and community that all help him reach his highest potential, but the importance of each of these three aspects has become clear to me and the avenues to maximizing the value of these different facets have multiplied through my research.

In all honesty, my attitude has also changed. I went into this project not expecting to find much. In my mind, I saw group homes as a rushed attempt to create an alternative in the wake of discontent with institutions: a solution to create something "better than before." However, I have learned that companies across the country are improving group homes and other housing solutions in unprecedented ways to strive for the best life for each of their residents.

As I learned in every interview I conducted, we need this change in attitude to happen on a national scale. If we can show people the immense opportunity in the field, the quantity of housing options can also grow. We desperately need more supply to meet the demand, and approaching the market through the lens of innovation may be just the way we get there.

In my last interview, I ended up speaking with someone completely separated from the disability field. Amanda Rosenberg is a senior UX and design researcher at Fitbit in San Francisco. She has a master's degree in design and an MBA from IIT Institute of Design and focuses on human-centered innovation with emerging technologies for both public and private sectors. She is also an alumna from my high school, so I decided to reach out to her about my book in the hopes that maybe she had a connection to the community. When we began to talk, she told me about her job and her process for doing research.

As a design innovator she completes a common practice dubbed the "design thinking process." While there are many different variations of the process, she laid out the four main steps for me:

1. To discover: "This is going in with the big broad questions and an open mind to understand the current state of things and some sort of trends and projections."
2. To conceive: "Based off of what we've learned, how can we address weaknesses."

3. To define: "What is the solution? Let's get really specific. Here are the priorities for what to design and create for your product or service."
4. To iterate: "This is the back-and-forth between creating and getting feedback and creating and getting feedback.... that continues even when something's out in the world."

All of the organizations outlined in the book are at some stage in this design thinking process. They are using the same techniques as innovators throughout the country as they work to improve the IDD housing market. Even so, everyone I spoke with for this book, had some connection to the field before innovating within it. It begs the question: Why is it not the other way around? Instead of people in the IDD housing field becoming innovators, why are there not more innovators entering the disability field?

I leave this task to everyone who reads this book. Get the conversation started about disability housing. Not just in the disability community, but with anyone who wants to make the world a better place. If there is not a drastic increase in disability housing services soon, the number of people who require supportive housing immediately and have nowhere to go will continue to multiply.

People's lives are on the line. My brother's life is on the line.

So spread the word.

We have a field which is begging for innovation, and there are so many amazing organizations ready to help anyone interested in getting involved.

If *Ability Innovation* has taught me anything, it is that a home is more than walls and a roof. It is possibilities: the possibilities for friendship and growth and happiness along with the possibilities for pain and fear and sadness.

A home is where you build your life, and everyone deserves to have that opportunity.

RESOURCES

CHAPTER 2: FINDING A HOME

Autism Housing Network: http://www.autismhousingnetwork.org/

- HQ: Gaithersburg, Maryland
- Database Available: Nationwide

CHAPTER 3: CREATING A HOME

Center for Independent Futures: https://independentfutures.com/

- HQ: Evanston, Illinois
- Consultation Available: Nationwide

Partners4Housing: https://partners4housing.com/

- HQ: King County, Washington
- Consultation Available: Nationwide
- Roommate Matching Service: Washington and Arizona

CHAPTER 4: CHOICE

Coalition for Community Choice: http://www.coalition-forcommunitychoice.org/

Together for Choice: https://www.togetherforchoice.org/

Point Rider, Inc.: https://www.pointrider.org/

- Consultation Available: Nationwide

CHAPTER 5: SMART HOME TECHNOLOGY

Imagine! Smart Homes: https://imaginecolorado.org/services/imagine-smarthomes

- Location: Boulder, Colorado

Living Resources Smart Home: https://www.livingresources.org/smart-homes/63-living-resources-smart-homes

- Location: Guilderland, New York

CHAPTER 7: PROCEDURAL DESIGN

MAGIC: https://magicinc.org/collaboratories/tech-innovation/health-smart-home

- Locations: Westminster, Maryland

CHAPTER 8: STAFF ATTITUDE

Living Services Alternatives: https://www.lsahomes.org/

- HQ: San Jose
- Location: Santa Clara and San Jose, California

CHAPTER 9: L'ARCHE

L'Arche USA: https://www.larcheusa.org/

- Locations: Alabama, California, Florida, Georgia, Illinois, Iowa, Kansas, Massachusetts, Missouri, New York, Ohio, Oregon, Pennsylvania, Virginia, Washington, Washington D.C.

CHAPTER 10: CHANGING THE HIRING POOL

Target: http://www.targetcommunity.org/

- Location: Westminster and Gaithersburg, Maryland

CHAPTER 11: INTENTIONAL DESIGN

Building Ohana: https://www.buildingohana.org/

- Developing Location: Spokane, California

Three Oaks Communities: http://www.salinemapleoaks.com/

- Developing Location: Saline, Michigan

CHAPTER 12: MIXED-USE COMMUNITIES

Camphill Village Association of North America in the USA: https://www.camphill.org/

- Locations: California, Minnesota, New York, Pennsylvania, Vermont

LTO Ventures: http://ltoventures.org/

- Developing Communities: Cincinnati, Ohio; San Antonio, Texas

CHAPTER 13: FUNDING AND COMMUNITIES

Flying Colors: https://www.flyingcolorsofsuccess.org/

- Location: Westminster, Maryland
L'Arche Boston North: http://larchebostonnorth.org/

- Location: Haverhill, Massachusetts

ACKNOWLEDGEMENTS

As this book is a medley of stories and experiences, I would first and foremost like to recognize all of the people who make up these pages. My amazing parents spent countless hours with me remembering and discussing Robb's housing journey. They were the ones who listened as I read my manuscript over-and-over and offered the praise I needed to persevere and the criticism I needed to improve the work up until the final draft. When the writing grind was getting to me, my brothers Robb and Poe were always there for a hug and a laugh. I could not be more grateful to my family for their unwavering support.

Thank you to Desiree Kameka, Pam Blanton, Mark Olson, Dana Hooper, Laura Goble, Judy Woodruff, Deborah Finck, Bill Godfrey, Michael Hardesty, Diana Giard, and Amanda

Rosenberg for sharing your stories and experiences with me and the readers of this book. You all are truly inspirational!

Thank you also to developmental editor Sherman Morrison, marketing editor Stephanie McKibben, copy-editor Chau Le, cover designer Krzysztof Famuła as well as Leila Summers, ChandaElaine Spurlock, Brian Bies, Eric Koester, and everyone else at New Degree Press who helped me turn my scattered stories into a published book!

To JaLynn Prince, Paul Conley, and Barry Horwitz, thank you for taking the time out of your day to provide invaluable feedback on my manuscript.

Thank you, the reader, for taking a step into the field of group housing innovation! I would like to especially thank the people who supported me in my pre-order campaign:

David "Cool Dave" Alexander, Claire Armbruster, Jane Avinger, Meredith Baker*, Lisa Bell, Joy Benenson, Jennifer Bishop, Cleo Braver*, Joo In and Roland Breitenecker, Melanie Brent*, Jean Brooks, Jeanette Budzik, Sophy Burnham, Ali Clark, Paul Conley, Keara Connelly, Jennifer Crowley, Susie Culp, Theresa Danos*, LaKerry Dawson, Janette Desmond, Marsha Derrickson, Margaret Diskin, Carla Douros, Mary and George Doub*, Siri Lise and Robb Doub*, Jason and Eliza Factor, Deborah Faryniarz, Charles Fenwick*,

Emily Fetting, Mary Kim Folds, Tyler Gearhart, Marie Gerwig*, Glen Gregory, Jaimie Griffin, Elizabeth Cochary Gross, Mark Grovic*, Meredith and Jay Harris, Amy Haugen, Kerry Haugh, Matthew Hetrick, Augusta and Gill Holland*, Siri and Gill Holland, Carrie Holloway*, Dana Hooper, Barry Horwitz, Shelly Howard, Marielise Jacobs, Jennie Jones, Daniel Kasper, Eric Koester, Ashley and Doug Kollme*, Astri and Barrett Kollme*, Jeff Koontz, Maria Lerner, Audrey Leviton, Kimmy Lin, Laura and Mike Maguire*, Laura Majka, Lizzy Tyler and Kent Majka, Beth McDonald*, Albert Michaels, Elizabeth O'Brien, Mark Olson, Jason Palmer, Wendy Pantle, Paul Pittman, Monica and Lasse Polmar, GQ Qaiyum, Rousby and Cathy Quesenberry, Charlotte Riggs, Kimberley Riley, Sue Sadler*, Leigh Luter Schell*, Ingrid and Bjorn Johnny Skaar, Inger Lise and Johnny Skaar, Mollie and John Spilman, Susan Stern, Janis Swindlehurst, Madelyn I.B. Tannen, Anabel and Peter Teuten, Jim Toya, Allie Tyler*, Poe Tyler, Katie Walsh, Courtney Watkins, Adam Whelchel, Diana White*, Elizabeth Wickware, Mary Wildeman, Casey Wilson, Dallas Wilt*, Ann Wopat, and Kendall Yim.

Thank you to all of the unsung heroes in the IDD field including Special Olympics Maryland, Camp Huntington, Athletes Serving Athletes, Team Up For 1, Walking Discovery, St. Elizabeth School, Ridgecroft, The Stewart Home and School, Kennedy Krieger, and Iteneris. Everything you all do to serve my brother and other individuals with IDD is nothing short of amazing, and we are all forever grateful to have your help and guidance.

In addition, I want to thank all of the people who have supported Robb and the rest of my family over the past twenty years. Especially Emma, Awele, Ms. Dupree, Caitlyn, Amanda, and Doug, we are so lucky to have you all in our lives!

To all of my teachers at The Bryn Mawr School and my advisors Ms. Park, Dr. Riley and Ms. Walsh: Thank you for giving me the tools to explore my passions and articulate my discoveries. I couldn't have written this book without you.

To all of my extended family, thank you for your support here and always. I especially want to thank my grandparents: Mormor, Bestepapa, Mary, and George, my aunts and uncles: Barrett, Astri, Gill, Augusta, George, and Rebecca, and my cousins: George, Tori, Freddie, Burns, Elizabeth, Shaw, Maya, Ellie, Cora, Lilla, and Owsley.

Finally, I want to recognize the people with IDD from past and present who require assisted living. Your stories have been in the dark for too long, and I hope I can play some small part in remembering and preserving your experiences so that we can one day achieve quality housing for all.

*Multiple copies

APPENDIX

INTRODUCTION

"Definition of Intellectual Disability ." *American Association on Intellectual and Developmental Disabilities,* 2019. Accessed September 9 2019. http://aaidd.org/intellectual-disability/definition.

"Census: More Americans Have Disabilities – Disability Scoop." *Disability Scoop,* 2012. Accessed September 9 2019. https://www.disabilityscoop.com/2012/07/26/census-more-disabilities/16111/.

Braddock, David, Laura Haffer, Richard Hemp, Emily Shea Tanis, and Jiang Wu. *The State of the States in Intellectual and Developmental Disabilities: 2017.* 2017.

Otterman, Sharon. "Schools Struggle Over How To Teach Severely Disabled People." *The New York Times, 2017.* Accessed September 9 2019. https://www.nytimes.com/2010/06/20/education/20donovan.html.

Merrill, Elizabeth. "The Game Nobody Could Forget." *ESPN,* 2016. Accessed September 9 2019. https://www.espn.com/espn/story/_/id/14780896/jason-mcelwain-changed-lives-inspired-autistic-community-20-point-game-10-years-ago.

"Heart Warming Moment – Homeless Man And Girl With Down Syndrome.". *ZOFA ViralWorld,* January 31, 2019. Accessed October 1 2019. https://www.youtube.com/watch?v=hmodj8eiCSo.

Braddock, David, Nicole T. Jorwic, Amie Lulinski, and Emily Shea Tanis. "Rebalancing of Long-Term Supports and Services for Individuals with Intellectual and Developmental Disabilities in the United States." *The State of the States in Intellectual*

and Developmental Disabilities Data Brief 2018, 2018. Accessed September 9 2019. https://www.colemaninstitute.org/wp-content/uploads/2018/04/SOS-Brief-2018_2_Rebalancing.pdf.

Bigby, C. and E. Bould. "Guide to Good Group Homes, Evidence about what makes the most difference to the quality of group homes." 2017. *Centre for Applied Disability Research*. Accessed September 14, 2019. https://www.cadr.org.au/images/1765/good-group-homes-fullguide.pdf.

CHAPTER 1

Dix, Dorothea. "The History of Mental Retardation, Collected Papers." *University Parks Press.,*1843. Accessed September 14 2019. https://www.disabilitymuseum.org/dhm/lib/detail.html?id=737&page=all.

Dix, Dorothea. "Astonishing Tenacity of Life." *Providence Journal,* April 10, 1844. Accessed September 14, 2019. https://sites.google.com/site/psychiatryfootnotes/case-histories-from-the-history-of-psychiatry/abram-simmons.

Wood, Andrew G. "Dix, Dorothea Lynde." *American National Biography,* 1999. Accessed September 14, 2019. https://doi.org/10.1093/anb/9780198606697.article.1500181.

"Make the Deviant Undeviant." *Parallels In Time: A History of Developmental Disabilities.* Accessed September 14, 2019. http://mn.gov/mnddc/parallels/four/4b/1.html.

Warder, Graham. "Franklin Pierce's 1854 Veto." *Disability History Museum*. Accessed September 14, 2019. https://www.disabilitymuseum.org/dhm/edu/essay.html?id=36.

"Howe's Speech In Batavia." *Disability History*. Accessed September 14, 2019. http://disabilityhistorywiki.org/wiki/index.php?title=Howe%27s_speech_in_Batavia.

Grenon, Ingrid, and Joav Merrick. "Intellectual And Developmental Disabilities: Eugenics". October 20, 2014. Frontiers In Public Health 2. Frontiers Media SA. doi:10.3389/fpubh.2014.00201.

Johnson, A. "The Segregation And Permanent Detention Of The Feeble-Minded." Journal of *Psycho-Asthenics,* March, 1906. Accessed September 14 2019. https://www.disabilitymuseum.org/dhm/lib/detail.html?id=1571&page=all.

"Buck vs. Bell Trial." *Eugenics Archive.* Accessed September 14, 2019. http://www.eugenicsarchive.org/html/eugenics/static/themes/39.html.

Wolfensberger, Wolf. "Changing Patterns in Residential Services for the Mentally Retarded." *President's Committee on Mental Retardation,* Washington, D.C. January 10, 1969. Accessed September 14 2019. https://www.disabilitymuseum.org/dhm/lib/detail.html?id=1909&page=17.

"From Training School to Asylum." *Parallels In Time: A History of Developmental Disabilities.* Accessed September 14, 2019. http://mn.gov/mnddc//parallels/four/4c/2.html.

"History Context–Leadership in the History of the Developmental Disabilities Movement." *Disability History.* Accessed September 14, 2019. http://disabilityhistorywiki.org/leadership/context.asp.

"Reasons Why Parents Organized." *Parallels In Time: A History of Developmental Disabilities.* Accessed September 14, 2019. http://mn.gov/mnddc/parallels/five/5a/6.html.

"1950 – 1970 Improve the Institutions." *Parallels In Time: A History of Developmental Disabilities.* Accessed September 14, 2019. https://mn.gov/mnddc/parallels/five/5b/1.html.

"1947 – 1980 The Parents' Movement." *Parallels In Time: A History of Developmental Disabilities.* Accessed September 14, 2019. http://mn.gov/mnddc//parallels/five/5a/1.html.

"Best Practices in Supported Employment." *Agency for Persons with Disabilities (State of Florida),* January 1, 2015. Accessed September 14, 2019. http://apd.myflorida.com/training/docs/2015 Best Practices in Supported Employment Manual Draft.pdf.

Brown, Dalton. "The Horrifying Truth Uncovered: Willowbrook State School." *Rooted In Rights,* October 15, 2014. Accessed September 14 2019. https://rootedin-rights.org/the-horrifying-truth-uncovered-willow-brook-state-school/.

Primo, Albert T., Executive Producer. *Willowbrook: The Last Great Disgrace,* 1972. SproutFlix. Accessed September 14, 2019. http://sproutflix.org/all-films/willowbrook-the-last-great-disgrace/.

"About Us." *National Council on Disability.* Accessed September 14, 2019. https://ncd.gov/about.

"ADA – Findings, Purpose, and History." *ADA 30.* Accessed September 14, 2019. https://www.adaanniversary.org/findings_purpose.

"Unlocked: The Lois Curtis Story." *Robin Rayne: A Souther Photojournalist's Notebook,* November 27, 2010. Accessed September 14, 2019. https://assignmentatlanta.wordpress.com/2010/11/27/unlocked-the-lois-curtis-story/.

"Olmstead v. LC: History and Current Status." *Olmstead Rights.* Accessed September 14, 2019. https://www.olm-steadrights.org/about-olmstead/.

"Institutions in Brief." *National Council on Disability,* 2012. Accessed September 14, 2019. https://ncd.gov/publications/2012/DIToolkit/Institutions/inBrief/.

CHAPTER 2: FINDING A HOME

"Your Service Coordinator." *Service Coordination.* Accessed September 14, 2019. https://www.servicecoord.org/resource-coordinator/.

"Family Supports Waiver Providers." *Maryland Department of Health Developmental Disabilities Administration,* January 4, 2019. Accessed September 14, 2019. https://dda.health.maryland.gov/Pages/FSW_Providers.aspx.

CHAPTER 3: CREATING A HOME

"Our Model." *LTO Ventures.* Accessed September 14, 2019. http://ltoventures.org/our-model/.

Living a Full Life: Jonathan's Story. Center for Independent Futures, April 27, 2015. Accessed September 14, 2019. https://independentfutures.com/overview/media-center/.

"Creating Housing Options." *Center for Independent Futures.* Accessed September 14, 2019. https://independentfutures.com/housing-options/.

Living a Full Life: Jonathan's Story. Center for Independent Futures, April 27, 2015. Accessed September 14, 2019. https://independentfutures.com/overview/media-center/.

CHAPTER 4: CHOICE

"Learn about the Issues." *Coalition for Community Choice.* Accessed September 14, 2019. http://www.coalition-forcommunitychoice.org/learn-about-the-issues/.

"Fact Sheet: Summary of Key Provisions of the Home and Community-Based Services (HCBS) Settings Final Rule." *Centers for Medicare and Medicaid Services,* January 10, 2014. Accessed September 14, 2019. https://www.medicaid.gov/medicaid/hcbs/downloads/hcbs-setting-fact-sheet.pdf.

"Guidance on Settings That Have the Effect of Isolating Individuals Receiving HCBS from the Broader Community." *Centers for Medicare and Medicaid Services.*

Accessed September 14, 2019. https://www.medicaid.gov/medicaid/hcbs/downloads/settings-that-isolate.pdf.

"Our Voices." *Coalition for Community Choice.* Accessed September 14, 2019. http://www.coalitionforcommunitychoice.org/our-voice/.

"Home and Community-Based Settings Regulation – Heightened Scrutiny" *Centers for Medicare and Medicaid Services,* March 22, 2019. Accessed September 14, 2019. https://www.medicaid.gov/federal-policy-guidance/downloads/smd19001.pdf.

Mendal, Scott. "CMS Issues New Guidance on its Settings Rule." *Together for Choice,* June 6, 2019. Accessed September 14, 2019. https://www.togetherforchoice.org/single-post/2019/06/06/CMS-Issues-New-Guidance-on-its-Settings-Rule.

DESIGN INTRODUCTION

Bigby, C. and E Bould. "Guide to Good Group Homes, Evidence about what makes the most difference to the quality of group homes." *Centre for Applied Disability Research,* 2017. Accessed September 14, 2019. https://www.cadr.org.au/images/1765/good-group-homes-fullguide.pdf.

CHAPTER 5: SMART HOME TECHNOLOGY

Herskowitz, Valerie. "Computer-Based Therapy for Autistic Children" *Organization for Autism Research,* January 1, 2003. Accessed September 14, 2019. https://researchautism.org/computer-based-therapy-for-autistic-children/.

"Power Wheelchair Drive Controls." *Mobilitybasics. Ca.* Accessed September 14, 2019. https://mobilitybasics. ca/wheelchairs/drivecontrols.

"What's In Your Cabinet?" *Then Again, What Do I Know?* October 10, 2018. Accessed September 14, 2019. https:// mark-thenagainwhatdoiknow.blogspot.com/2018/10/ whats-in-your-cabinet.html.

"Smart Homes: An Emerging Real Estate Opportunity" *Coldwell Banker.* 2018. Accessed September 14. *2019.* https:// blog.coldwellbanker.com/wp-content/uploads/2018/01/ CES2018-Smart-Homes-An-Emerging-Real-Estate-Opportunity.pdf.

Muselman, Dannette and Elizabeth Woodruff. *Changes in Quality of Life for Group Home Residents of the Bob and Judy Charles SmartHome: An Exploratory Analysis.* University of Colorado Denver, November 2010. Accessed September 14, 2019. http://www.ucdenver.edu/academics/ colleges/medicalschool/departments/pediatrics/research/ programs/psi/Resources/Documents/Smarthome%20 Research.pdf.

Kovner, Josh. "Bill Would Encourage Housing Options For Group Home Clients." *Hartford Courant,* March 23, 2018. Accessed September 14, 2019. https://www.courant.com/

news/connecticut/hc-news-group-home-housing-alter-natives-0324-story.html.

"Smart Homes." *Living Resources.* Accessed September 14, 2019. https://www.livingresources.org/smart-homes/63-living-resources-smart-homes.

"Designing a Wearable System for Prevention of Health Care Worker Injuries." *Xsens.* Accessed September 14, 2019. https://www.xsens.com/customer-cases/wearable-system/.

"Why Build Alexa Skills?" *Amazon Alexa.* Accessed September 14, 2019. https://developer.amazon.com/en-US/alexa/alexa-skills-kit.

Farr, Christina. "'Alexa, find me a doctor': Amazon Alexa adds new medical skills." *CNBC,* April 4, 2019. Accessed September 14, 2019. https://www.cnbc.com/2019/04/03/amazon-alexa-hipaa-compliant-adds-medical-skills.html.

CHAPTER 6: DESIGN EMPATHY

Connell, Bettye Rose, Mike Jones, Ron Mace, Jim Mueller, Abir Mullick, Elaine Ostroff, Jon Sanford, Ed Steinfeld, Molly Story, and Gregg Vanderheiden. "Principles of Universal Design." *National Center on Accessibility,* April 1,

1997. Accessed September 14, 2019. http://www.ncaonline.
org/resources/articles/universal_design.shtml.

Winters, Wendi. "Home of the Week: Home sweet home for
four developmentally disabled residents and their caretakers." Capital Gazette, March 28, 2015.

"AJ Paron-Wildes :: Design Empathy – Hatch Festival 2013."
Hatch Experience, February 22, 2014. Accessed September
14, 2019. *https://www.youtube.com/watch?v=enxyBFflSmA.*

Cherry, Kendra. "Positive and Negative Afterimages." *Very-
Well Mind,* June 22, 2019. Accessed September 14, 2019.
https://www.verywellmind.com/what-is-an-afterim-
age-2795828.

CHAPTER 7: PROCEDURAL DESIGN

"MAGIC's Smart Home Presentation 8/28/2017." *MAGIC,*
August 31, 2017.Accessed September 14, 2019. https://www.
youtube.com/watch?v=E9Co4fz5ykE.

Staff/Resident Relationships Introduction

Bigby, C. and E. Bould. "Guide to Good Group Homes,
Evidence about what makes the most difference to the
quality of group homes." *Centre for Applied Disability*

Research, 2017. Accessed September 14, 2019. https://www.
cadr.org.au/images/1765/good-group-homes-fullguide.
pdf.

CHAPTER 8: STAFF ATTITUDE

Berens, Michael J. and Patricia Callahan. "In the rush to
close institutions, Illinois glossed over serious problems
in group homes." *Chicago Tribune,* December 30, 2016.
Accessed September 14, 2019. https://www.chicagotribune.
com/investigations/ct-group-home-investigations-ci-
la-met-20161229-htmlstory.html.

Berens, Michael J. and Patricia Callahan. "In Illinois group
homes, adults with disabilities suffer in secret." *Chicago
Tribune,* December 30, 2016. Accessed September 14,
2019. https://www.chicagotribune.com/investigations/
ct-group-home-investigations-cila-met-20161117-html-
story.html.

Bigby, C. and E. Bould. "Guide to Good Group Homes, Evidence about what makes the most difference to the quality
of group homes." *Centre for Applied Disability Research,*
2017. Accessed September 14, 2019. https://www.cadr.org.
au/images/1765/good-group-homes-fullguide.pdf.

CHAPTER 10: CHANGING THE HIRING POOL

"Staffing Shortages For Direct Support Professionals (DSPs)" *eWeb Schedule,* September 30, 2018. Accessed September 14, 2019. https://ewebschedule.com/staffing-shortages-for-direct-support-professionals-dsps/.

"As moderator of the first National Forum on Disability Issues today in Columbus, veteran broadcast journalist Judy Woodruff has a personal stake in the discussion." *The Columbus Dispatch,* July 26, 2008. Accessed September 14, 2019. https://www.dispatch.com/article/20080726/entertainment/307269832?template=ampart.

Zirpoli, Tom. "Nonprofit View: McDaniel graduate program and Target Inc. work hand-in-hand." *Carroll County Times,* April 15, 2018. Accessed September 14, 2019. https://www.baltimoresun.com/maryland/carroll/opinion/cc-op-nonprofit-target-20180329-story.html.

Henderson, Nancy. "Right on Target: The Target Community and Educational Services Program Gives Graduate Students Crash Course in the Realities of Working with Individuals with Disabilities." *The Exceptional Parent,* September, 2008. https://www.questia.com/magazine/1G1-186900954/right-on-target-the-target-community-and-educational.

"The Science of Caregiving, Brining Voices Together." *The National Institute on Nursing Research*. Accessed September 14, 2019. https://videocast.nih.gov/vodCaptions/ninr080717.txt.

COMMUNITY RELATIONS INTRODUCTION

Lauber, Daniel. "Impacts on the Surrounding Neighborhood of Group Homes for Persons With Developmental Disabilities." *Governor's Planning Council on Developmental Disabilities,* September 1896. Accessed September 14, 2019. http://www.planningcommunications.com/gh/illinois_impact_on_surrounding_neighborhood.pdf.

Holloway, Lynette. "For Group Homes, No Easy Victories; Year After Year, Communities Rebuff the Mentally Retarded." *The New York Times,* July 18, 1995. Accessed September 14, 2019. https://www.nytimes.com/1995/07/18/nyregion/for-group-homes-no-easy-victories-year-after-year-communities-rebuff-mentally.html.

Tribou, Doug. "Creating A Community For People With Developmental Disabilities." *NPR,* February 4, 2018. Accessed September 14, 2019. https://www.npr.org/2018/02/04/583095407/creating-a-community-for-people-with-developmental-disabilities.

CHAPTER 11: INTENTIONAL COMMUNITIES

"About The Foundation for Intentional Community." *Foundation for Intentional Community*. Accessed September 14, 2019. https://www.ic.org/foundation-for-intentional-community/.

"Housing Options for Individuals with Disabilities: Intentional Communities." *M&L Special Needs Planning*, May 2, 2013. Accessed September 14, 2019. https://specialneedsplanning.net/2013/05/housing-options-for-individuals-with-disabilities-intentional-communities/.

CHAPTER 12: MIXED-USE COMMUNITIES

"Camphill Village Copake, New York." *The Camphill Village Copake Foundation*, June 3, 2013. Accessed September 14, 2019. https://www.youtube.com/watch?v=EDiqBEEK6yE&t=153s.

"Let Each Light Shine: A Portrait of Camphill Village." *The Camphill Village Copake Foundation*, July 6, 2016. Accessed September 14, 2019. https://www.youtube.com/watch?v=LY4okUIXIOI.